NARROW GAUGE RAILWAY SCENES

Adolf Hungry Wolf

Artwork, Maps and Back Cover
by John Coker

Winter Night Steam in Durango

(Facing page) Readying a steam engine in below-zero weather expresses powerful elements in narrow gauge railroading; challenges of man's machines against the forces of nature. Rarely do such events occur anymore on today's surviving narrow gauge trackage, but here in Durango during 1961 the battle was still on, with No. 494 scheduled to take a freight south through high desert country to Farmington, New Mexico.

(This page) On the same evening, D&RGW Hostler Ed Kettle stands by the 1882 embossed heater in the Rio Grande's Durango roundhouse, taking care of the engines, keeping steam up, doing the servicing. "Pa" Kettle was a proud man who had worked for some time on the Marshall Pass line before it was closed.

Both photos, Richard Steinheimer

(Front cover) Narrow gauge mixed train on Guatamala's IRCA blasts out of town at Mazatenango in August 1964 behind Baldwin-built 2-8-0 No. 108, headed up the mainline for the branch to Champerico. Regular passenger train at left has just pulled in from the Mexican border, bound for Guatemala City behind a Baldwin 2-8-2.

Photo by Adolf Hungry Wolf, with David Riggle

Copyright © 1992 by Adolf Hungry Wolf
All rights reserved. This book may not be reproduced in any way.
Information and additional copies available from:
Canadian Caboose Press, Box 844, Skookumchuck, B.C. V0B 2E0
Book design - Adolf Hungry Wolf
Typesetting and Layout - Communications Plus
Printed and bound in Canada by Kromar Printing Ltd.
First Printing - 1992

ISBN 0-920698-41-7

(Above) A mixed train heads out of downtown Mexico City in 1964, commanding respect from traffic at the crossing, even if little attention from the two old timers down in the courtyard. This scene has changed completely since then, with narrow gauge trains gone and the area covered by modern high-rise buildings.
AWH photo

(Opposite) Here's narrow gauge railroading of a much different sort in California's Sierra Nevada forests, away from big cities. Michigan-California Lumber Company Shay No. 5 has just finished the day's work at Pino Grande, back in the autumn of 1937.
Railway Negative Exchange/AHW collection

Contents

Introduction

Wander with me from the scene on our front cover, showing narrow gauge station life in rural Guatemala as mixed train meets mainline passenger, to the mountains and valleys of Colorado, through the forests and down the coast of California, then to Pennsylvania and North Carolina coal country, stopping by a couple of Maine two-footers on our way up to Canada's Newfoundland, over to an Ontario stone quarry, then west to Alberta and British Columbia for lines that are only memories, plus a famous Shay and some tankers that still run.

There exists an unusually large body of published work about narrow gauge railroading in general, which indicates that many people enjoy such books and articles. There is a lot of support and encouragement among enthusiasts of narrow gauge trains to write down what they know and to print up their pictures. Taking this as a cue, I started about 30 years ago to assemble a little trove of interesting stories and photos on the narrow gauges myself. That's what helped bring about this volume.

Although a sizable body of photographic record exists for narrow gauge railroading, few document actual life at the stations and in the roundhouses, or aboard engines and cars; often a 3/4 front view of a train with smoking locomotive was considered the ideal shot. I've tried to select photos for these pages based on their visual appeal as well as their historical value, hoping that you'll find much to enjoy even in those otherwise undramatic "still life" photo studies, such as the scenes of quiet yards, buildings and sidings. Photos like these are often all that remain today.

This book's main purpose is to provide entertainment, not to delve into historical and technical matters that have probably already been presented more than once in publications bigger and better than this one. If this volume ends up on the same shelves as those time-honoured ones, I'd feel satisfied. Perhaps it'll serve as inspiration at times when you're not certain just which of those bigger texts to open up. There's a little of most every notable narrow gauge operation from the last 50 years or so shown on these pages, with some of the places still operating today. After you've made sort of an "armchair circle tour" through here, maybe you'll get out on one of the real narrow gauge trains for a trip of your own.

Among those who have helped me in putting together this book, I'd like to give my appreciation to the following, in no particular order: Warren E. Miller, Railway Negative Exchange; W.C. Whittaker; Richard H. Kindig; Otto Perry; Robert W. Richardson; R.V. Nixon; Johnny Krause; Richard Steinheimer; Elmer Treloar; John S. Anderson; Timothy S. McCartney; James A. Brown; Robert J. Sandusky; Robert D. Turner; Ernie Plant; Dick George; Ward Kimball; John Poulsen; Fred Hust; Sam King. Also my son Okan, the most avid companion in our family for making narrow gauge trips. A special thanks to our friend John Coker, a modern-day "boomer" in real narrow gauge railroading (C&TS and D&SNG), who stayed aboard my caboose - CPR 436788 - while we spent four days and nights talking non-stop narrow gauge, going over the pictures and captions for this book. He also did the artwork back home in Durango, where he's an artist when not at work as an engineer or something else on the narrow gauge.

3/93

3

The Colorado Narrow Gauge Circle

Southwest of Denver, Colorado lies a system of narrow gauge railroad grades whose geographic outline looks like a lopsided map of the United States. At one time you could go down from Denver to Salida, then travel for the next few days and nights through the Rockies aboard various narrow gauge trains, eventually getting back to Salida without ever having gone to any place more than once. Called the Narrow Gauge Circle, this trip was widely promoted back in the days when people sought adventure through train travel. It was a photographer's dream - fantastic scenery and remarkable railroading. A few hardy individuals took up the challenge to document what they could, their work having since been often seen, their names well recognized. Such is the magic of that Circle that even now, decades after it was first broken and years since most of the track was taken up, those of you viewing these pages will still find interest and pleasure in them. Had we been around to charter the "Nomad" or the "Edna" sometime during the first decades of this century, these are the kinds of scenes we might have viewed from their observation platforms.

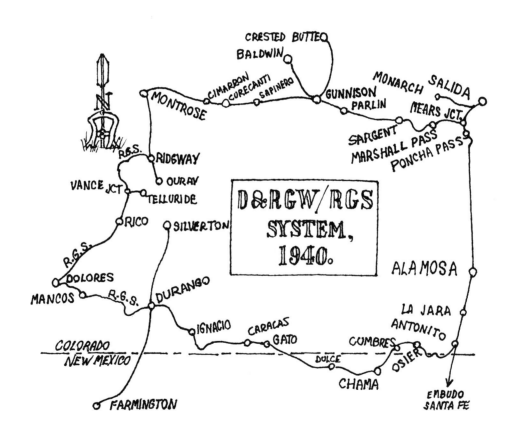

(Above) The spirit of narrow gauge railroading is captured in this scene at Rico, Colorado, a setting as if from a fairy tale, one of many enchanting destinations on the Narrow Gauge Circle. It is the summer of 1951, the slopes are nearly bare of snow. The photographer has aimed his camera at Rio Grande Southern No. 20, just arrived with its light train from Dolores, Colorado. Even though the distance was only 35 miles, poor track conditions forced a general 10 - 15 mph speed limit, making it about a three hour trip. Rico was one of four terminals on the Rio Grande Southern, the hub of mining and ranching operations that supplied trains with traffic until highways came and moved things much quicker. To this day Rico is one of the few remaining examples of a partial ghost town left in the San Juan Mountains. Of this scene, only the water tank remains. However, the photographer ended up in charge of this engine, but that's another story...
Robert W. Richardson photo

Five Days of Colorado Narrow Gauge in 1947
With Ward Kimball

"I will never forget that famous Colorado narrow gauge trip of July 1947! Six days of sheer ecstasy in three 1880s D&RG coaches, plus open gons and a caboose, using five different locos! It was all organized by Nolan Black of the L.A. 'Railroad Boosters,' also known as the Pacific Railroad Society. As an interesting note, our group of 67 took 66 rolls of colour, 328 rolls of black and white, plus 100 rolls of movie film.

"We left Alamosa, Colorado on July 16 behind D&RGW No. 473, which brought us to Durango. The next day, No. 463 took us to Silverton along with its regular mixed train. The Rio Grande Southern part was especially memorable, hauled by RGS Ten-wheeler No. 20. The trip was filled with music, food, drama, scenery and lots of laughs. The best excursion my wife Betty and I ever experienced on a narrow gauge railroad."

(Opposite) This memorable 1947 excursion started here in Alamosa, where a D&RGW clerk is seen at the standard gauge/narrow gauge assignment board while a couple of obviously-steam crewmen keep him company.

(Left) Engineer and Conductor of the special train compare watches by the cylinder of No. 473.

(Below) Passengers stretch their legs and look for camera angles as the special train stops for water at Cumbres, on the way to Durango.
Both pages, Ward Kimball photos

Durango in 1947

(Above left) Camera and film equipment of another era was used to record narrow gauge scenes from the dome car "Silver Vista." Looks like Betty Kimball has spotted something in her viewfinder that the fellows are missing out on.

(Far left) "I took over 125 four by five negs on this trip," says the photographer, "plus plenty of 16 mm film!" Here's his shot of the conductor with an unusual right-of-way sign.

(Left below) At Durango, the excursion passengers find No. 452 on switching duty.

(Above) Inside the Durango depot, an operator types out train orders using the hunt and peck method. That extra chair sports some pretty fancy footwear.

(Right) Looks like No. 463 got a recent coat of shiny black paint on her flanks, maybe to dress up for the special excursion that she'll be leading up to Silverton on this day.

Both pages, Ward Kimball photos

(Above) Stopped on the way to Silverton, Engineer W.N. Squires looks from the cab window of D&RGW No. 463 while Fireman R.D. Schock stands in the gangway, sporting sunglasses and red bandana, right in style for the visiting California crowd.

(Above left) While the engine takes water at Needleton, some of the passengers snap photographs and others quench their thirst from a mountain stream.

(Left) The four boxcars behind No. 463 carry Silverton freight, but the gondola is for the tourists, who also rode in the baggage car, coaches and caboose.

(Above) Back in Durango the following morning, Rio Grande Southern's beautiful Ten-wheeler No. 20 smokes it up by the coal tower, ready to haul the excursion passengers over the RGS line to Rico.

(Above right) A group portrait with No. 20 during a pause on the RGS route. The shot was taken with a self-timer, since the photographer is also in the scene, kneeling fifth from left with white circle on his cap.

(Right) Oldest and youngest photographers on the trip. Retired Southern Pacific engineer W.E. Butler prefers a tripod for his folding Kodak, while young Jimmy Row hand-holds his "modern" twin-lens reflex.

Both pages, Ward Kimball photos

(Above) Conductor J.C. Phillips lights the vintage kerosene lamps in one of the excursion train's coaches.

(Above left) No. 20 and the special train, parked in front of the RGS depot at Dolores. In less than five years this line will be shut down.

(Left) Imagine travelling 863 miles of track in this narrow gauge coach, sharing the rhythms and adventures through the long days and nights. The photographer says they had to sing pretty loud to overcome the noise of the car wheels on Rio Grande Southern roadbed. Among the interesting passengers was noted railroad artist Harper Goff, crooning his heart out on the left. Photographer's wife Betty is in the foreground on the right.

((Right) From Rico to Ridgeway the grades were considered too steep for No. 20, so the special was hauled by 2-8-2 No. 455, sporting a medium sized plow and a new set of white flags. Here they meet the regular train service, as provided on this day by Galloping Goose No. 5. The fans know they are witnessing a fading episode in Rocky Mountain railroading, as each picks out a spot from which to record it.

(Below) Again the fans are scouting for photo angles; those who are closest trying to get out of this shot, while some further back are getting the higher up views. This was truly a fine train to behold, to ride on and to document.

Both pages, Ward Kimball photos

To Alamosa by Boxcar in 1933

Northern Pacific telegrapher Ronald Nixon put his employee pass to good use over the years by travelling throughout North America to document train activities with his cameras. The resulting work has been widely published in books and magazines, starting in the 1930's. I recorded the following story some years ago when he gave me these prints.

"In May of 1933 I went by train from Missoula, Montana to Denver and from there to Montrose, where I transferred to the narrow gauge D&RGW for a trip to Alamosa. As our train pulled into Montrose on May 9 behind standard gauge 4-6-0 No. 769 we were met by narrow gauge Consolidation No. 320 with four wooden cars. Although not actually tiny, they sure looked small next to our train. I took some pictures while No. 320 pulled ahead with one of her two baggage cars; I checked afterwards to make sure my suitcase had been switched aboard. Six others transferred here into the two coaches besides myself. I was the only one with a camera and they did look at me a bit strangely. Not too many young fellows in suit and tie took pictures of trains in those days.

(Above) "Here's the scene at Montrose on May 9, 1933 about five or six minutes after we arrived. The engineer of my incoming train is oiling his Ten-Wheeler, while No. 320 gets ready to bring me to Salida."

(Below) "A close up of our narrow gauge motive power finds the engineer propped in his window., waiting for the loading of mail, baggage and passengers, before bringing us along the Gunnison River to Salida. Too bad much of the trip through the Black Canyon and over Marshall Pass was at night. By the way, not long after this trip, No 320 was wrecked and scrapped."

"My destination on this trip was Ala-mosa, but when we got to Salida the next morning I learned that there wouldn't be anything but a freight leav-ing for many hours. I asked the freight crew about catching a ride with them, but they were afraid to get caught; in those days the railroad could fire a guy over something like that and he'd lose out on his pension. But they offered me a boxcar, so I accepted it instead. The first part of the ride went well; I even managed to get a few pictures. But when we stopped at the bottom of Poncha Pass I made a big mistake. The crew asked me if I wanted to go up on the first trip or second, as they had to double the train from there up to Poncha Pass (to haul it up in two sections), each time doubleheaded. I decided to go up on the first run, figuring to look around on top of the pass and get a few pictures, which I did. Finally it got onto darkness and they still didn't show up with the second half of the train, including both engines and the caboose. It was getting quite cold so high in the mountains and I had no means for starting a fire. I was dressed alright, but as a travelling rail fan, not as a mountaineer. It turned out they had troubles of their own - broken couplers and train in two - so they never showed up until well after dark, with me nearly frozen. To top it off, I still had to ride my boxcar to Alamosa, with the night air blowing cold drafts through cracks I hadn't before noticed. When we got to Alamosa at about 4:00 a. m. I couldn't even talk. I just made signs to get a room at the hotel and it took me about three hot showers before I felt warmed up!

(Top) "D&RGW Extra 492 stands at Poncha Jct. in the afternoon of May 10, 1933, ready to doublehead with the first half of its train up to Poncha Pass."

(Centre) "Looking from my boxcar door on the way up to Poncha Pass, our helper has just gone ahead across this wooden trestle, not trusted to hold both engines at once. A brakeman rides at the front of our engine, waiting to couple back up on the other side."

(Bottom) "It was fantastic when we reached Poncha Pass. The sun was out and I snapped a couple of pictures, before the engines went back downhill for the rest of our train. It was dark and cold before I saw them here again."

Both pages, R.V. Nixon photos

ALAMOSA 1933

(Left) "*Since my vocation has always been to photograph different kinds of engines, I found my visit to Alamosa to be a lucky one since I caught Ten-Wheeler No. 174 still in their shop. Most of their early engines were being discarded or scrapped at this time. I don't know if this one ever made it back to work or for how long.*"

(Below left) "*Here's No. 473 outside the Alamosa shops on May 11, 1933, back when she was only 10 years old. A lot of people think she's way older than that.*"

(Below right) "*Mudhen*" *No. 460 was parked up ahead of 473 that same time still wearing a massive plow from winter service.*
All three, R.V. Nixon Photos

"*You'd think that freezing trip over Poncha Pass cured me of freight trains, but I rode another boxcar from Alamosa back to Salida - and even with the same crew! But this time I wasn't alone; I shared the car with five Mexicans, and at first they seemed like a pretty rough looking bunch. In those days I didn't smoke but I always carried a 10¢ pack of cigarettes. If there were hobos around, I'd give them the smokes and that usually made them friendly. In the case of these Mexicans, they just about adopted me right there. They were cooking some coffee in a can and it looked like pretty evil stuff - dark and thick enough to float a piece of lead. There were even sticks floating on the surface. But I knew if I turned them down I'd lose the friendship, so I accepted. That was as good of coffee as I ever had!*

"*These fellows all had instruments with them, besides their bedrolls, so I was entertained with wonderful Mexican music while we battled up the grades. Unfortunately, the boxcar was partly filled with loose ties, the most dangerous thing to ride on. Every time there was a brake application we'd all get thrown to the other end. But we made it through alright.*

"*This time when they doubled Poncha Pass I stayed at the bottom till the second trip. At the top I asked them if we'd reach Salida in time for me to connect with the Denver passenger train. They said "no," except for the helper engine, which was to run ahead of the freight in D&RGW fashion. So I talked the helper crew into letting me ride their cab; they weren't much enthused, but finally agreed. We just got to Salida in time too, as my train pulled out about five minutes later. After three hard days and nights on the narrow gauge I just got into my coach seat and collapsed; I never knew a thing until we reached Denver.*"

(Above) Engineer to fireman: "Say Charlie, are you sure that fellow you got the back up signal from was our conductor? This here caboose seems mighty low for a mainline haul." Narrow gauge Caboose No. 0517 is being switched over Alamosa's dual gauge trackage by standard gauge No. 1161. Narrow gauge 490-series engines were rebuilt from engines similar to this but of the 1000 series. In the background is a tender in work train service.

(Below) Intergauge: Another mixing of the gauges - a custom not often photographed - is this case of narrow gauge Mike No. 494 hauling a couple of clean Rio Grande 40 foot standard gauge boxcars on the dual gauge trackage east of Alamosa in 1950. Known as the "Antonito turn," the train also features idler cars to join the different gauge couplers and a narrow gauge caboose on the rear.
Both, Robert W. Richardson photos

To Chama and Durango by Train in 1962

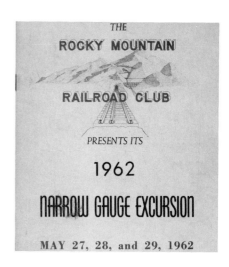

(Opposite page) It might have been just another in a long line of excursion trips over "the narrow gauge" for older members of the Rocky Mountain Railroad Club, who sponsored a Memorial Day weekend run from Alamosa to Silverton in 1962. But I was still in high school, so for me it was the trip of a lifetime. My first visit to this surviving remnant of the fabled narrow gauge circle. I never set foot in Chama or Durango until our train pulled up to their stations. I'd never even been to the Colorado Rockies before, much less experienced the thrill of standing trackside as a doubleheaded narrow gauge train thundered through them with clouds of smoke and steam. In this case, our train is making a photo runby at dramatic Windy Point, the weather at the time living up to its name. No. 491 helps our train's freshly painted No. 487.

(Below) Being a holiday weekend, I was warned not to expect freight traffic, though I dearly yearned to see just one real narrow gauge freight train. We left the dual-gauge yard in Alamosa early that morning and tackled Cumbres Pass before noon. Suddenly, out through the open window and up on the nearby hillside, I spotted a pair of steam engines, sitting quietly at the head of a string of flatcars. A Doubleheader! Out of nowhere, like a dream. My first thought was: I'll never see it again - our train seemed to be going away from it. Instinctively, I snapped a picture. But a few minutes later we doubled back, our engine working hard upgrade, until we coasted to a halt on a siding next to that freight. Some of us got off to witness this meeting of real working narrow gauge trains high up in the Colorado Rockies. In the photo we see No. 483 rolling her string of flatcars slowly past our 11-car Rocky Mountain Railroad Club excursion train near the summit of Cumbres Pass. The freight's helper engine, No. 484, has already been cut off and is headed downgrade towards Alamosa on its own. And yes, that is fresh snow on the slopes in late May.
Both, AHW photos

(Above) At 10,015 feet our excursion train has reached the top of Cumbres Pass and pulled up to the water column in front of the Cumbres station. No 487's tender has just been refilled, so we're ready to continue.

(Left) Fourteen miles downgrade from Cumbres we have reached Chama, where train crews change and our engine is serviced. This view looks eastward at the action from down at the Durango end of the yard. In the days of smaller locomotives, it took about four of them just to haul a 15 car train up to Cumbres, so this scene would have been alive with smoking engines back then.

(Above) Our Memorial Day excursion train arrived at Durango's classic station after dark, at the end of a very long and tiring day. Our re-entry into the modern world was announced by the flickering images of a drive-in movie that we passed on the outskirts of Durango. It was an interesting contrast, our seats aboard the 1880s train and the seats of those gathered within their cars to see the show. Different forms of travel and entertainment, briefly catching each other's eyes.

The Durango station was built in 1882 and has changed little on the outside since then. Among its colour schemes was a complete coat of dark red; white with green trim; and since the 1940s a "depot buff" with dark red trim. At one time a trolley line terminated on the station's street side. The Rio Grande Southern had its headquarters upstairs during the final years of that railroad's operations. This view was taken from the roof of a boxcar and shows part of the roundhouse at right, water tank in the distance. At this time the station still provided Railway Express Agency service, as seen by the truck with cigarette advertisement at the left.

(Below right) Two heirlooms of the Colorado narrow gauge lines greeted 1962 excursion train passengers from within their fenced compound behind the roundhouse. Although the high mountain Silverton Northern RR had been shut down since 1941, its unique little "Casey Jones" railbus appears to have survived quite well on its Cadillac chassis. It has since been moved back up to Silverton. At left is the 1878 business car "Nomad," which is now available for charter service on the Durango & Silverton.

Both pages, AHW photos

(Left) My wish to see a narrow gauge freight during our 1962 Memorial Day weekend excursion came more than true as we ended up having three different meets, including this one with No. 491 leading an eastbound freight through the trackside community of Gato (Spanish for cat). A branch from here to Pagosa Springs got pulled up some years before. Nowadays the tracks are gone from Gato as well, but the water tank and other buildings are still maintained.

(Above) Leaving Gato, No. 491 leads her freight along the banks of the San Juan River, headed for Alamosa to pick up another load of oil pipes with the flat cars and gons. Pipe traffic provided important income for the narrow gauge throughout the 1950s, but to a much lesser extent by the time of this photo.

(Below) What's the matter cowboy, narrow gauge got you worn out? After three long days of travel aboard wooden cars through the Rockies, only the most hardy still had their cameras out. Among them were such noted narrow gauge old-timers as R.H. Kindig, Bob Richardson, Otto Perry and others.

All three, AHW photos

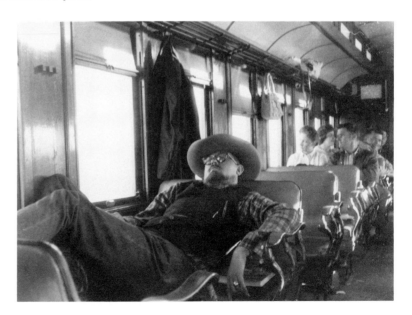

Exposing Film
with Otto Perry

(Right) Noted train photographers are often besieged by fans who want to get similar pictures, perhaps hoping that by standing nearby with their own cameras the skill and magic will rub off. But here in this 1962 Chama scene is the Colorado master himself, Otto Perry, standing center foreground pretty much by himself, waiting for No. 491 to back into No. 487 and its eastbound Rocky Mountain Railroad Club excursion train. On his shoulder was a leather bag for photo equipment, in his hands a big black camera with a set of bellows more patched up than the boiler of a K-27. I looked at that picture machine as another would look at a brush in the hands of Rembrandt. Like narrow gauge railroading itself, he represented a nearly bygone era. I value this occasion when we exposed film on the same subject.
AHW photo

(Below) When I sent Otto Perry a print of the picture with himself, he replied by sending the shot he took. It shows some of our fellow travellers chatting and visiting with train crews in the final minutes before departing from Chama to begin a doubleheaded assault on Cumbres Pass with 11 cars.
Otto Perry photo

Winter on the Narrow Gauge

(Left) It's a cold zero degree (fahrenheit) morning east of Chama as the photographer captures his son Alan (on snowshoes) and family dog Shadow in line with Mikado No. 494 working upgrade with a hill turn for Cumbres, hauling one-quarter of an eastbound freight which will be assembled at the top of the pass. There's another 2-8-2 pushing on the rear, as well.

Richard Steinheimer photo

(Below) A Christmas card scene on the Rio Grande Southern during the winter of 1950. RGS No. 20 is making a caboose hop as an extra train at Stoner, Colorado because the line's Roadmaster wanted tracks cleared of snow for his "Work Goose" No. 6. The caboose is RGS 0404, known affectionately as "Ophir-Ophir." It was purchased by the photographer soon after this scene and is now at the Colorado Railroad Museum, along with No. 20, which was bought by the Rocky Mountain Railroad Club.

Robert W. Richardson photo/John Coker Collection

(Opposite top) The last big snowplow operation by the D&RGW took place in March 1962, as Rotary OY stood steamed at Antonito, ready to clear heavy snow on Cumbres Pass. Power for the train is provided by Mikes #483, 487 and 488. Also in the consist are a flanger and several outfit cars.

T.K.S. Brewster photo/AHW Collection.

(Opposite, below) Rotary OM is being demonstrated on a rail fan special three miles out of Chama on the morning of Feb. 15, 1976. After working all day, the train got only as far as Lobato Trestle. The Cumbres & Toltec Scenic Railroad has both surviving narrow gauge rotaries, which have been used several times on the line in recent years. On this occasion, engines 487 and 483 are pushing (the rotaries are not self propelled) while a caboose, two outfit cars and a gondola provide space for some 100 rail fans who came along on the trip. Leaning from the Rotary's pilot house door at front is C&TS Superintendent John Oldberg. Working as engineer is Master Mechanic Bernie Watts (leaning out of the engineer's window) while Fireman John Coker is seen leaning way out of the gangway between the rotary and its tender, checking the smoke from his fire.

C.J. Pease photo/John Coker collection

Firing the Rotary Plows
with John Coker

"Working aboard one of the rotary plows in deep snow is probably the closest one can get nowadays to the real spirit of old time steam railroading in the Rocky Mountains. It is exciting - a lot is happening - with bells, whistles and all the other steam noises; keeping the injector operating; water dripping down everywhere from constant melting ice and snow; the smells of coal smoke and valve oil cooling on the hot machinery.

"The two surviving narrow gauge rotaries are both at Chama; I have fired them altogether on five different trips. Although quite old, they're still in good shape because they were not used much over the years - not even every winter, depending on snow conditions. Rotary OM was built by Cooke Locomotive and Machine Co. in 1889, while OY was built by Alco in 1923. They spent most of their lives assigned to Alamosa and Chama - one stationed on each side of Cumbres Pass. OM is generally preferred over OY because it cuts better into heavy packed snow.

"Because of their blade speed, these rotaries consume a great deal of coal and water. They are similar to firing an engine, but more of a challenge because of the heavy consumption. Once you are on the apron and begin the job of firing a rotary, you are out of touch from everyone, including the engineer. You have no idea what is going on up ahead and very little time to look outside. You just keep shovelling coal into the firebox, your work being guided by the steam pressure gauge and the waterglass. Even the engineer can't see much - he receives signals via a bell system from the pilot house. It is the pilot up front who serves as eyes for the crew.

"The rotaries have their own whistles, which signal the engineers on the locomotives that are pushing. The rotaries are not self propelled. They are still used occasionally for opening up the line over Cumbres Pass."

The "San Juan Express"

(Right) The "San Juan Express" was Colorado's last daily narrow gauge passenger train, offering reserved seats, on-board meals and rear end parlour cars until its final run in January 1951. In this scene, No. 485 leads the train with four cars west of Chama.
Fred Hust photo

(Above) Here's the "San Juan" running eastbound a few miles out of Durango, climbing into Wilson Gulch. This may have been just before Christmas, when increased passenger traffic required more than the usual four or five cars (seven in this case). The cold weather helps make combined smoke and steam vapors from the engine more dramatic.
AHW collection

(Below) Eastbound "San Juan" with No. 483 meets its westbound counterpart at the usual place (when both trains were on time, at 1:35 p.m.), the 39 car siding at Carrracas, Colorado, some 56 miles east of Durango, on May 28, 1950. The cook in his apron waits for a family to get on.
Bob Andrews photo/Tom Klinger Collection/from John Coker

(Above) Here's the "San Juan Express" Train No. 215 near the very end of its days, at Cumbres on January 22, 1951. Mikado No. 473 is showing off its new tourist/Hollywood look, which some considered quite appealing while others called it a sacrilege. This engine and Consolidation No. 268 were both painted Rio Grand gold at this time as an experiment in paint schemes for passenger locomotives. In addition, No. 473 was given a diamond stack and early style headlight, which company P.R. said was "to backdate the engine to its original 1890s appearance." Trouble is, the engine wasn't built till 1923. No. 268 kept its "gold" paint job till long after retirement, while No. 473 went back to "basic black" soon after this. However, she and her two sister 470s were fitted with similar stacks until the Durango and Silverton took them over and restored their traditional appearances. Incidentally, if you've been to Cumbres and photographed a scene somewhat like this (as you still can at times) you may wonder why the building looks so different. This depot was torn down soon after passenger service was suspended; today's Cumbres depot is actually the old section house. Track on right was for storage of work equipment and bad order cars.

Robert W. Richardson photo/from John Coker

Branchline to Santa Fe

The so-called "Chili Line" (named for the popular red and green chili beans grown along the way) was a 125 mile branch connecting Santa Fe with Alamosa and Denver through a junction at Antonito. At the start of the 1880s the D&RG made plans to run this narrow gauge line clear down to Mexico City, but that grand dream was soon scuttled. Instead of becoming an international narrow gauge mainline, the branch struggled for survival until its closure in 1941. Had the future tourist potential of the beautiful route between Taos and Santa Fe been recognized in those early World War II days, the tracks might have survived to make an adventurous shuttle run between two world famous artistic towns and places.

(Left above) Mixed train No. 426 stopped daily, except Sundays, here at Embudo, New Mexico for station business, water, and usually for a scheduled meet. Tracks on this Branch were heavy enough to allow the use of 2-8-2s like No. 471, seen on May 10, 1940. This was one of the engines taken to Alaska a year later by the Army and wrecked.
R.H. Kindig photo

(Left below A cold winter day in Santa Fe, as No. 478 waits to depart from the D&RGW depot on January 16, 1937. Snow on the engine pilot and men with thick jackets, hands in their pockets, assure us that it was a cold day in spite of the sunshine and bare station grounds. There was still freight and passenger service to Santa Fe by two railroads, the narrow gauge D&RGW from the north and namesake AT&SF from the south. The handsome brick depot survives today as a restaurant with fantastic atmosphere, near the heart of town.
Paterson-George collection

(Opposite above) Southbound train No 425 paused at Embudo with mail car 63 and coach 306. It's July 2, 1941 - in a few more weeks train service on the branch will end. The Embudo depot became a noted landmark after H.W. Wallace became the agent there in 1912. For 22 years he gathered stones and piled them around the depot building, turning it into one of the most unique structures on any narrow gauge line. Most of the stones came from the Rio Grande riverbed, but some were brought and sent to Wallace by friends from far away. This station is now a restaurant and the water tank is still standing.

(Opposite below) The same train is seen at Santa Fe ready to make the eight hour trip back to Antonito, where passengers can connect with the "San Juan" for Alamosa and points beyond. Says the photographer: "The train is seen backing up to its terminal. The D&RGW wye, coaling and engine shed was about five blocks away, at the north edge of Santa Fe; after unloading, the train backed to that point for servicing. When riding it, one had a chance to get a shot of it running if one hustled down the track, or else waited for it in the morning and then hurried to the station to get aboard. The crew were all high on seniority and knew everyone. Traffic was very light; a few passengers between stations; railfans were about the only through passengers. The line followed the Rio Grande River from Otowi to Embudo (about 28 miles) , then went up seven miles of 4% grade to Taos Jct, where they used to have a stage connection for Taos itself. A lumber branch took off near there going to La Madera for a few years from 1914 to 1923. The rest of the route wound across empty sagebrush country with lots of pinon trees. This was the highest part of the line; storms from Cumbres Pass area would sweep viciously across causing deep drifts, sometimes blocking the line and requiring a rotary plow to reopen. Spanish was spoken by most of the people in that area and the coach had signs in both languages. Little of the line had ballast; mostly just dirt. The Railway Post Office would exchange small bags of mail for remote places; recall one bag being brought by a boy of about 12, riding a horse."
Both, Robert W. Richardson photos

Chama, New Mexico

(Below) The same setting, some 43 years earlier, showing the arrival of No. 473 with the daily "San Juan Express," in this case five cars, at a time when trains still provided Chama its main connections with the outside world, on September 9, 1946. Cars on the train include Nos. 119, 126, 312, 323 and parlour car "Durango," which is now at Knott's Berry Farm.

Robert W. Richardson photo

(Above) The same train on a clear day in December 1950, this time with only four cars but heavier motive power. No. 484 continues to reside in Chama.

Dennis O'Berry photo/Ted Wurm Collection

(Above left) Trading centre, railroad division point and helper station, Chama has kept most of its original railroad atmosphere, including this sign on the depot.

AHW photo

(Opposite) An autum night at the Chama depot finds No. 487 just in with a freight, replaying a frequent scene at a vintage location. Except for a few details, this photo might be from 1949, or even 1899, though it was actually on the occasion of a photographer's special, just after the annual Narrow Gauge Convention of 1989.

A&OHW photo

Chama East - *With a Helper*

(Left) The early morning sun cast a long shadow on the switchstand just beyond the old enginehouse at Chama when I took this picture through its doorway in the Summer of 1965. There's no action out in the yard yet, just strings of wooden cars sitting still, plus three engines steaming quietly; only the hostlers are busy going around getting things ready for today's freight movements. A load of ties is heading east on a string of flat cars, to be hauled by Mikado No. 487, (seen here), taking No. 493 along as helper. The two crews are booking in right now, while an earlier crew is about to take No. 492 for a trip west to Durango. The photographer and his friend Jim Kreider flipped a coin to decide which of the two trains to follow, driving a rented car and being quite short on time. I shot this photo with my father's Voightlander Vitessa on 35 mm Agfa film and he liked the results. He and his father were both photographers in Switzerland (we all carried the same first name); they were my motivation for capturing some of these scenes.

(Above right) The first sign of life that summer morning comes when No. 492 is backed out onto the mainline and taken to the tank for water and to the coal tower for fuel. Uphill, the town of Chama is just starting to wake up, though this is years before tourists so it'll be just another typical day. Everybody can hear the railroad going about its business, but the hungry flocks of passengers are still in the future, along with the resulting change of economy.

(Below right) Looking back toward that open doorway at the enginehouse while standing on the coal dock, we see No. 487 still simmering alone in the foreground, while No. 492 hooks a caboose to the back of its train, down by the depot. Looks like a fresh load of ties going in that direction too, attesting to timber work in the Chama area. This photo was made with a well-worn 2 1/4 x 3 1/4 Speed Graphic camera, whose home-developed sheet films tended to give some scenes a more aged look. The effect was somewhat like putting sunglasses on.

Both pages, AHW photos

(Left) Wedge plow at the front of No. 487 seems out of place on this warm summer morning, like a parka or snow boots, but it won't be long before the white stuff blankets Cumbres Pass again, hiding the narrow gauge tracks in between the passing of trains. On today's trip over the pass the plow might still come in handy if any rocks have tumbled onto the grade.

(Right) The big yellow water tank at the east end of Chama's yard fills No. 487's tender, as the hostler gets the engine ready for the freight train crew. Still in service, this tank makes a popular focal point for photographing arriving and departing trains.

(Far right) Hot, dusty and back-breaking is the hostler's chore of cleaning ashes from beneath the locomotive fireboxes. Here, No. 487 is parked strategically over the ashpit from which the cooled remains of previous trips will later be shovelled into the waiting gondola.
Both pages, AHW photos

(Left) The hostler has a precarious perch at the bottom of the Chama coal tower as he holds the chain that controls coal flow from the chute into No. 487's tender. This mighty wooden structure is officially called a "75 ton Balanced Bucket Mechanical Coal Tower," one of three built by the D&RGW during an upgrading of facilities in 1923-24. It is the only one left standing, though generally out of use since the end of freight operations. C&TS crews one time brought an engine here during the 1980s when they were in a hurry to get on the road and didn't want to wait for a late coal delivery truck. They filled the tender of their locomotive alright, but then the chute broke and the coal wouldn't quit coming out! They couldn't move the engine forwards because it wouldn't clear the engine cab, nor backwards because of the dog-house on the tender. It took a long time to wedge a plug into the chute and get the coal out of the way, a lot of which was by then all over the ground. There had been a suggestion to separate engine and tender to get them out of the way, prompting one noted wag to wish he could have had a shot of a big narrow gauge Mike steaming through Chama with only the front, minus tender. In that regard, John Coker recalls the time visiting Hawaiian 2-4-2 No. 5 was steamed up and run a bit, then separated from its tender before the engine was run into the shop for work.

(Above) Here's another of those larger format sheet film shots whose gritty appearance might let it pass for a scene from the 1940s instead of the summer of 1965, so timeless was the vintage environment at Chama. The two eastbound engines have now been fueled and watered so they're about ready to tie on to their train and get rolling. Helper 493 is being used for some last minute switching, while the boss of road engine 487 probably figures each ounce of oil is worth a pound of cure, as he puts a few more drops on the valve gear. The canvas water bags dangling below cab windows will come off their hooks several times before the day is done, as things heat up inside for the crews. Note the variations in engine details, including snowplows, domes and other appliances. Engine 487 was built new in 1925, whereas No. 493 had already served for years as a standard gauge 2-8-0 before being rebuilt like this in 1928.

(Opposite) Here's No. 493 up at the east end of Chama yard looking ready to head east, though this is actually just a switching move and she'll end up on the rear end of the train before it departs. In those days some choice pieces of antique rolling stock, such as the express car in back, seemed doomed from rough use in work train service, though now in more recent years many of these have been rebuilt to preserve their valuable heritage.

Both pages, AHW photos.

Head-End and Tail-End

Making a Charge on Cumbres Pass

(Facing page) By the mid-1960s most railroading in North America was modern and diesel, so it seemed incredible to watch this scene of two steam engines working hard, hauling an every-day freight train of old wooden cars over a rugged mountain pass on a mainline railroad in the summer of 1965. It was as if someone had forgotten to turn a page of history; a train that had somehow been left behind. No. 487 is shown eastbound for Alamosa with a load of new ties and a few boxcars, sister engine 491 pushing on the rear.

(Right) Being in the cupola of this caboose had to be a memorable ride, though company and crews generally frowned on having outsiders aboard. This steep S-curve, a few miles out of Chama, continues to provide a fantastic setting in which to photograph trains charging uphill on the Cumbres & Toltec Scenic Railroad.
Both photos, AHW

Far left) A single boxcar, seven flat cars of fresh ties, nine more boxcars, plus the caboose - an 18-car train - requiring two engines to get up the four percent ruling grade of Cumbres Pass.

(Upper left) These cows have given up their grazing to run from the approaching iron horse, up on the grassy western slopes of the Colorado Rockies, as No. 487 darkens the sky overhead with coal smoke.

(Lower left) One cannot forget the memorable sight of two steam engines working hard to lift their train from the valley bottom, up past the rock formations of Windy Point, the sounds of their whistles echoing across the scenic wild countryside. So it has been, right here, for over 100 years. Who knows how many thousands have been thrilled to partake of this drama with their eyes, ears, hearts and cameras.

(Above) At the very top of Cumbres Pass - 10,015 feet - the hardest work is over, as the crew stands down on the ground for some fresh air. The train is just cresting the grade outside the old Cumbres section house, nowadays thought of as the depot. After taking water at the standpipe, No. 487 will pull ahead and do some switching with the train while helper 493 cuts off at the back end and takes its turn under the spout. It's cool way up here, even on this otherwise hot summer day in 1965. Scents of pine trees and other plants mingle with those of the panting coal burner. Mountain birds provide symphony music along with the whispers of wind. And of course, there's always No. 487, hissing, roaring, clanking; the gladiator of this cast.
Both pages, AHW photos

(Above) With the train out of the way, No. 493 pulls up to level track for her watering, while the immense wooden snow shed that covers the wye track stands silently in witness. Last active structure of its kind on the narrow gauge, the Cumbres snow shed collapsed some time after this 1965 view and has not been rebuilt.

(Left) Cooling off at Cumbres Pass! Just hearing all that water splashing down into the tender has a good effect; a few minutes to relax, have a cigarette, put things in perspective. On this day the elderly brakeman perched on the back platform of the caboose has just told a good joke about the conductor at a recent card game; the fireman is standing on the spout and having a laugh. With the tender full, No. 493 will drop off the caboose for the train, then run solo downgrade, clear to Alamosa, getting there well ahead of the freight.

(Above) Meanwhile, the rest of our eastbound freight out of Chama is leaving some of its boxcars here at Cumbres and picking up others recently emptied by the section gang. A lot of the freight being hauled these days is just for the upkeep of the old narrow gauge line. This photo shows how the scene might have looked with that train my friend and I were following in 1965. Even John Coker thought that's what it was; but this was actually taken right after the Narrow Gauge Convention at Durango in 1989! It is an example of going back to a place and getting a photo you've always wished you'd gotten "back then." The fireman and brakeman in 1965 were friendly fellows; I enjoyed standing nearby, being made to feel welcome, soaking it all in. I paid no attention to the freight being switched at this famous summit place nearby. Today's Cumbres & Toltec scenic operation provided another chance.

Both pages, AHW photos

(Above) The Old Man's ready to go! Conductor of eastbound freight waits patiently for fireman of helper Mikado No. 493 to fill the tender at the Cumbres water spout so they can get out of his way and let him get back to work on his caboose. The brakeman's right arm shows how easy it is to reach the roof of this petite car while standing on the front platform to watch the watering. At this point our time ran out on the rented car (a great luxury for a couple of 21 year olds!) so we left the eastbound train at Cumbres and rushed back to Durango to see about that westbound. The photo essay ends here, because the westbound got into Durango just ahead of us and all we got was a shot of No. 492 being put away in the roundhouse. It was the last time I saw the line under D&RGW ownership.
AHW photo

(Above right) All who've been to Cumbres will find this scene familiar, even though the photo was taken in July 1939, before most of us were born. There's a certain atmosphere about this place that comes just at the mention of the name Cumbres. The station and at least some of the cars in this photo are gone, along with trailing engine No. 485, but lead No. 484 is still a favorite on the C&TS.
R.H. Kindig photo

(Below right) The "San Juan" passenger train has stopped at Cumbres in August 1941 behind No. 475, which was taken away to Alaska the following year by the U.S. Army, never to return to these mountains.
Railway Negative Exchange/AHW collection

Chama to Cumbres in the Cab
With John Coker

"About nine in the morning you arrive at the yard in Chama and find the crew waiting in the depot for you, expecting to see your smiling face. A few minutes later the power for the day is brought down the mainline from the water tower by the hostler. After he finishes cleaning the cab he turns the engine over to you. As you set your grip under the seat you check the water glass first thing, then you open the firebox door to see if there's any clinkers.

"When the brakeman signals, you horse the Johnson bar back towards you (that's the big one on the floor), whistle three short blasts, release the engine brake (with the small brass handle), and gently pull out the throttle (the long bar coming out of the boiler). A couple seconds later the engine moves with a lurch.

"Once the engine is moving, you shut the throttle off and coast into the train. A good engineer can do this smoothly. After the joint is made, the brakeman connects the air hoses and charges the train with compressed air. You sit and wait while the trainmen inspect the train, then you perform a brake test which lets you know that all brakes are in working order.

"As the passengers begin to board and departure time nears, you fill the oil cans and set out to grease the running gear and spring rigging of the locomotive, inspecting at the same time for any defects in the engine. Meanwhile, the fireman is building a head of steam for the steep climb ahead, shovelling coal into the firebox and working the injector.

"When the highball is given, you reply with two long whistles, kick the Johnson bar forward with your foot and open the cylinder cocks (which are also foot operated). The fireman starts ringing the bell as you pull back on the throttle. Enveloped in steam and smoke, the engine moves its train forward. As it gathers speed, you notch the Johnson bar back towards you a little at a time so the steam moves more efficiently through the valves. About the time we pass the coal tipple and water tank we perform a running brake test by setting the air. When the conductor signals that the brakes are working on the train, you release the air and away we go.

"Chama yard ends in a grove of cottonwoods and soon the mainline brings us to the bridge over the Chama River, where you whistle a long and a short in warning. The iron truss rods of the old bridge clank loudly as the engine goes by, adding to the noise inside the cab. Your full concentration is demanded by the many aspects of operating the engine and train. Later there will be time to enjoy the trip, but for now you better watch your gauges, speed and the handling of the train behind.

"As you approach the first road crossing you observe conditions, watching especially for speeding vehicles and other possible dangers. The fireman works the bell and you whistle the standard two longs, a short and a long. Shortly after this crossing the engine reaches the foot of the grade where the real work begins. From here on it's an almost continuous 4% grade for the next 14 miles, which is steep railroading anywhere including the narrow gauge.

"The fireman is shovelling coal furiously to keep the pressure up to 190 lbs. per square inch, an amount we both check regularly on the steam gauge. He then gets his water injector going, which will run constantly now for the next hour. You pull the throttle out all the way and advance the Johnson bar two notches. The engine begins labouring hard as it works the train upgrade, the inside of the cab filled with noises of the exhaust from the stack, plus the rumble of wheels and the slapping open and shut of the firebox door. The fireman's shovel crashes into the coal time and time again. The rhythm of all these deafening noises actually makes you feel as one with the machine.

"As glowing hot cinders rain down all around you, the wheels start to slip and the rhythm is interrupted with a burst of extra loud noise as the engine shudders. Instinctively you reach to shut off the throttle and at the same time turn on the sanders, which reinstates the rhythm. You reopen the throttle quickly so as not to lose the momentum and possibly stall on the grade. The engine is working very hard, even though the train is moving at less than 10 mph.

"A white post with a black W on it reminds you that the train is approaching a station, so you whistle one long and look back for a signal from the conductor. When you get a highball, you whistle two shorts - meaning you're not going to stop there - after which you roll through the open field at Lobato. The grade is flat here for a short ways, so you back

off the throttle. Speed limit across Lobato Trestle is 10 mph. Doubleheaded trains stop and part here due to weight restrictions, with the helper going across the steel trestle alone, followed by the road engine and train.

"The grade starts up again right after Lobato trestle and the steep climb is uninterrupted for the next few miles. We enter the state of Colorado at Cresco and pass an old water tank which has been restored. Occasionally, upgrade engines still stop here for water when pulling heavy trains. After this we traverse several S-curves around rocky cliffs, then pass the railroad phone booth at Coxo. Above to the east you can see the rails climbing way up around legendary Windy Point.

"You whistle again for a highway crossing, this time at a spot often cluttered with cars of photographers who consider this one of the best spots along the narrow gauge. They can shoot close-ups of the train as it passes by here, then about 10 minutes later get a fantastic panorama of the train rounding Windy Point.

"At the head of the valley below Windy Point the rails curve over a high fill across Wolf Creek; the final and most spectacular couple of miles to Cumbres lay just ahead. At Windy Point the passengers and train crew are rewarded with a commanding view of the Chama valley, which you unfortunately have no time to enjoy because the demands of running the engine are crucial here. First, you have to whistle a long and three shorts to signify that the train will stop at the next station - with everyone but you listening to the whistles echoing off the mountain sides at this point. As a good engineer, you will get your injector going because you know that the one on the fireman's side will invariably overheat about now because of continuous use. You also need to back off the throttle here for a particularly sharp curve which has a permanent slow order of 10 mph. When you know that the last car of the train is past this curve you pull the throttle clear out again for the final few hundred feet to the summit.

"When the Cumbres section house (generally thought to be the station) comes into view you tell yourself that there's only a little ways left to go for this hard work. Approaching the water plug, you carefully work both your train and engine brakes so that you come to a smooth stop with the tender hatch spotted for water. As you stop, the pop valves lift to a deafening roar of excess steam. You secure the brakes, check to make sure various valves and the throttle are shut off, after which you step down with a sense of relief to stretch your legs, inspect the locomotive's running gear, and enjoy the cool mountain air after that hot session in the cab."

Dulce, N.M.

(Right) The Jicarilla Apache people have their headquarters at Dulce, which was served by this plain wooden station along the narrow gauge tracks. Here's No. 488, steaming westbound during one of the final winters, with the station already closed and its operator gone for good.

Tom Klinger Collection/from John Coker

(Below) Dulce had regular mainline passenger train service with the "San Juan" until 1951, when the D&RGW was given permission to drop the service. However, the New Mexico Public Utilities withheld its permission, particularly on behalf of the Apaches, so that for six months a mini "San Juan" was operated daily between Chama and Dulce. An engine and single combine sufficed to handle the virtually non-existent traffic. Here is Train #216 being backed to the Dulce depot from the wye at Lumberton, a few miles back,. Rio Grande gold was being applied liberally at this point, as seen on combine No. 212 and 2-8-2 No. 473, which also carried its new "Hollywood stack" and headlight. Notes the photographer: "The hearing to cancel this short train was held at Santa Fe on May 20, and very quickly the Commissioners gave their assent. The railroad officials decided that the train of that day would be the last. Word however didn't reach the crew before they left Dulce, so they didn't know it was the final run until they pulled into Chama and were told. I drove from Santa Fe to take pictures of this final run, but as the train was moving I found no way to tell them it was the last run until arrival at Chama."

Robert W. Richardson photo

Lumberton

(Above left) Freshly painted No. 487 has just arrived at Lumberton, N.M. with her eastbound passenger extra, headed slowly towards the siding for a meet with a westbound freight
AHW photo

(Above right) The freight has a mixed consist that includes new steel pipes headed for the gas and oil fields down the Farmington branch. Shutters click as No. 484 picks up speed, although many of the extra's passengers are too tired on this third day of their Rocky Mountain Railroad Club excursion to get off the train, which is stopped in the Lunberton siding.
AHW photo

(Lower left) Doubleheaded and thundering out of Alamosa with a westbound freight are 2-8-2's 481 and 483 (leading). It's January 1961, with a lot more snow in the mountains up ahead than is indicated by the few patches lying here among the blurred clumps of sagebrush.
Richard Steinheimer photo

(Lower right) Heading towards Alamosa about a year later, we see No. 491, paced at a steady 30 miles per, which wasn't much in our car but must have been a relief to the crew after their slow mountain climbing. The brakeman has his doghouse door open up on the tender, catching fresh air and stretching his legs for the ride. The helper engine of this freight rolled by here alone just a few minutes earlier.
AHW photo

The Farmington Branch

(Opposite page) Winter snow lies sparse across the mesa country of northern New Mexico as a narrow gauge freight train rumbles north towards Durango on the 45 mile Farmington Branch in the 1960s. Old 491 has a banged-up cylinder jacket and a couple of conspicuous patches on her tender, while the wooden cars behind haven't seen much of the carpenter; signs of the times, with the branch itself nearly out of business.

(Left) Farmington, N.M. was not the most exciting destination along the D&RGW, even near the end, when there weren't many choices.

(Below) The Farmington Branch originally ran on standard gauge out of Durango, expected to become a link with main line routes headed east and west. It was perhaps North America's only standard gauge line to reverse the trend and become narrow gauge later. Towards the end of its years the branch had a short burst of business with gas and oil developments during the 1950s. For several years almost daily freights forwarded bulky loads of long pipes that came to Alamosa from the mills in Pueblo. By the time these two shots were taken in the late 1960s, traffic down the weed-grown branch had ceased; the strings of cars were orphaned, some later to be scrapped, others sold and preserved. Railroading in Farmington is now just a memory, but it still gets hot and dusty there.
All three photos: Richard Steinheimer

Durango, Colorado

"In the days when the narrow gauge capital of the universe was Durango," said the widely travelled Lucius Beebe, "its yards were the mecca of the faithful to whom railroading is a major preoccupation regardless of hour or season." It may be that other places in the world also claim the honour of being a narrow gauge capital, but none have been more colourful or long lasting than Durango, Colorado. Even the name has romantic appeal, and the local depot is still at the heart of town. Steam powered trains can be seen there today, coming and going steadily. Every home in the well populated region can hear the soulful whistles; music for the heart, not to mention the economy, which is heavily supported by streams of tourist passengers.

(Right) Although the Durango depot is rightfully associated with the Denver & Rio Grande Western Railroad (notice the logo above the station signboard), for many years it was also used by the connecting Rio Grande Southern, whose unique Galloping Geese were among the strangest motive power to stop here. On this cold morning around 1940 (with snow on part of the depot roof and in the hills behind) Goose No. 4 is ready to depart with a load of mail for the isolated communities along the RGS line.

(Below) Looks like everyone's gone home for the day. Tomorrow's Silverton train is ready outside the depot, with observation car "Silver Vista" at one end and caboose 0587 at the other. All that remains to be done in the morning is to back the freight cars onto the caboose. The regular cars for this train are wearing Rio Grande gold paint schemes; presence of the four cars in dark green indicates that tomorrow's train may have an extra load of tourists. The caboose was built in 1900, rebuilt in 1942, then sold to the Flying Dutchman RR at La Porte, Ind. in 1966.

(Opposite) For over one hundred years, narrow gauge trains have sat in front of this same depot in Durango, waiting to head out into the hills and mountains. Built in 1882 when tracks first arrived, the depot's outside appearance has changed very little, even as the town and railroad both evolved through several different eras. Originally there were only horses and wagons where the Model A and tarp-covered truck sit on this summer day in 1947. For some years in between, a streetcar line came here as well. Today the place is so busy you can hardly park there at all. But this scene is from an earlier time, when life was less rushed and crowded. The engineer of No. 476 does a last bit of oiling before heading out of town with the "San Juan," while the conductor has a few words to say, maybe discussing train orders or giving some helpful advice, else sharing a funny incident that will keep the hoghead humoured for the next few miles.

Three photos, AHW collection

(Above) Here's the Silverton Mixed waiting in front of the Durango depot in August 1947 behind 2-8-2 No. 453, whose crew is about to have their final briefing as the uniformed conductor strides up with train orders. Looks like two loads of coal ahead of the caboose and passenger cars, as a crewman with 2-8-0 No. 315 stands by on the adjacent track to continue yard switching.
John Horan photo

(Left) Long time Durango resident No. 464 was captured in the late afternoon sunlight during October 1951, steaming softly and facing No. 478 at the sand house.
RNE/AHW collection

(Right) Here's an engine that might still be running out of Durango with its sisters today, if the U.S. Army hadn't requisitioned it during World War II and then worked it to death on the White Pass & Yukon. Taking water at the far end of the yard in August 1941, No. 472 had just a few more months here before the draft board struck.
RNE/AHW collection

(Below) Another ill-fated member of that class, No. 470 waits at the Durango depot to depart eastbound with the "San Juan" in February, 1938, before anyone here thought about a war that would require good narrow gauge engines. Across from the depot stands the Southern Hotel, an old railroad flophouse that advertises "Rates by Week or Month" and the luxury of "Cold water in every room." The Century Liquor Store downstairs offers "20¢ wine." In the snowy parking lot of the depot we see the distinctive snout of a Hudson "Terraplane." The old hotel is now a parking lot, with flophouse types a distinct minority in town.
RNE/AHW collection

(Below right) Heading out of Durango with an eastbound freight in the summer of 1965 is No. 493, of a stronger class that wasn't taken by the army. Although still within town limits, this scene shows how quickly the narrow gauge began to blend in with nature upon leaving the yard.
AHW photo

(Left) D&RGW caboose No. 0505 was originally second No. 6, built by D&RG shop crews in June 1886, receiving the number 0505 during a general caboose renumbering in 1887. The car has a 25 foot body and a total length of exactly 30 feet. Rebuilt in 1923, it is seen here at Durango in a fresh coat of boxcar red paint around 1950, while regularly assigned to long time conductor Myron Henry. This is one of two original D&RGW cabooses still in service at Durango.
Fred Hust photo

(Below) The yard at Durango, c. 1930, with fairly new No. 482 taking water at the tank, while one of the 490s heads out of town as helper on an eastbound freight. The photographer composed his shot to include somebody's vegetable garden and team of work horses in the foreground, while tracks near the roundhouse further back are filled with horses of the iron sort.
A.M. Payne Collection/from John Coker

(Above) Considered by many to be a queen among narrow gauge engines, Rio Grande Southern No. 20 is seen here in the summer of 1947 on the ready track near Durango's coal tower. The Schenectady-built Ten-wheeler was bought second-hand in 1916 from the Florence & Cripple Creek Railroad, a short-lived gold hauler connecting the two mining towns of its corporate name. At the time of this photo, No. 20 was freshly painted with a green boiler jacket for a Rocky Mountain Railroad Club excursion over the RGS out of Ridgeway. Two years later she was given an even fancier paint job for a starring role in the movie "Ticket to Tomahawk."
Paterson-George collection

(Right) The "San Juan" has just arrived at Durango with parlour car "Chama" on the rear. Built in 1880 by Jackson & Sharp, this was originally chair car No. 410, given the name "Camp Bird" in 1902, finally rebuilt as the "Chama" in 1937, one of three parlour cars used on the passenger train. The car was later sold to Knott's Berry Farm and rebuilt as a combine.
Fred Hust photo

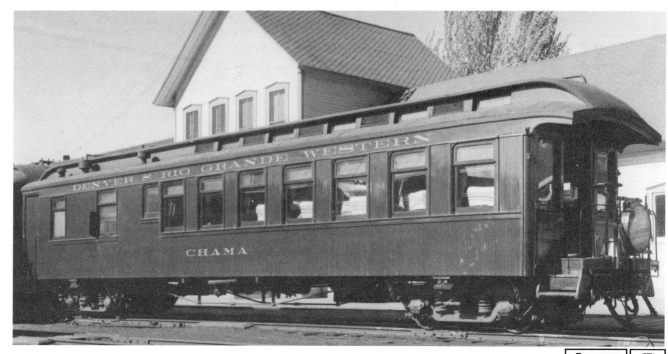

No. 453
The Durango
Switcher

(Opposite) It's a rainy spring morning in 1941, as the engineer and fireman of No. 453 wait by the depot for the arrival of a freight from Chama. Built in 1903, the engine appears still well-maintained, although soot covers everything including the men. On the front deck lies a spike hammer and part of a broken board, both no doubt used regularly while switching old cars on well worn tracks. Although the wide footboards at each end are mainly useful for standing on during yard movements, the brakeman's doghouse on the tender reminds us that this old veteran was still seeing some mainline service as well.

(Above right) Ten years later in the summer of 1951, Mikado No. 453 is again seen on switching duty at Durango. Notice that she has gained a handy toolbox which is mounted on the cab roof ahead of the doghouse. It's early in the morning; probably the Silverton train is being made up. Adding the caboose must be the next move, since lone cars are not left parked on the mainline in front of the depot for very long. The engineer is waiting for a signal from his crew, who are taking a sunny break underneath the station signboard. Wonder what antique metal items are in among those two gondolas full of scrap sitting at the left? Maybe stuff from ghost towns and railroad places that many museums nowadays would gladly display. But then, No. 453 is herself in that "late and lamented" category, scrapped just a few years before her historic value was fully recognized.

(Below right) In memory then, to her long and often photographed career, here is a sunny portrait of No. 453 parked outside Stall 4 at the Durango roundhouse, a little later that same 1951 morning. It was her moment of glory, witnessed in silence by four sisters sitting in the shade nearby. From left to right we have Nos. 464, 463, 42 and 20, all of them working for the Rio Grande Southern at that time.

Ironically, while the star of this photo is gone, the other four engines survive, though only one of them at this location. The structure itself of course burned down and was then rebuilt, with the turntable at the foreground still in use.

Three photos, Railway Negative Exchange/AHW Collection

(Left) Three cars for head-end business plus two for the passengers make up this Fourth of July "San Juan Express" in 1938, ready to depart from Durango behind ill-fated No. 477.
Otto Perry photo

(Opposite) Every photographer has a few special shots that really seem to capture the essence of their subjects and this is one of mine. It was a hot midday in August 1965 as I sat on a knoll at the edge of Durango, watching the departure of this eastbound freight train for Chama. The elevated view was not only best for shooting a train with the sun overhead, but it also brought much of the Durango yard into the picture. From left to right are the car shops, coal tipple, water tower, roundhouse and station, everything needed to service the Denver & Rio Grande Western's fleet of 2-8-2s that still performed steady service from here in three different directions. Today's mainline freight includes eight flat cars of new ties, two loaded gondolas and a string of boxcars back to the caboose. The fireman's down on the apron with his shovel, starting to put a little dent into the big pile of coal in the tender. Nowadays when I enter Durango on the modern highway that cuts through here, there's a feeling of satisfaction in having witnessed this scene while it still existed.
AHW photo

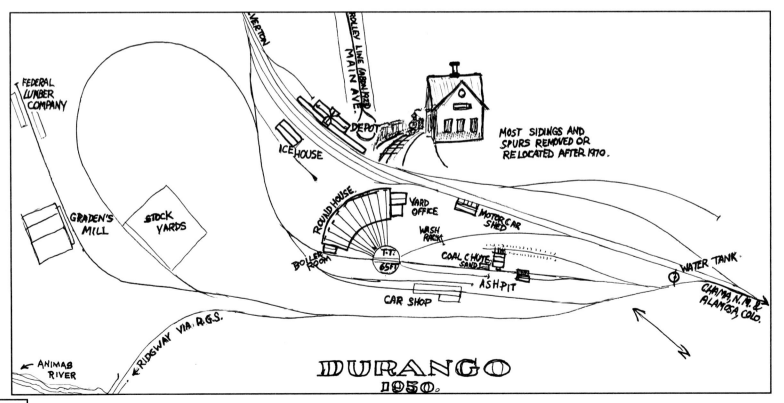

DURANGO
1950.

Durango
In the Sixties

(Opposite above) The car shop in Durango was still pretty busy in 1962, when this picture was taken. The D&RGW narrow gauge freight car roster numbered some 1,200 vehicles, including 298 box cars, 252 stock cars, 213 gondolas, 159 side dump coal cars, 20 open-end gondolas (for pipe service) and 266 flats. Also on the line were 41 private tank cars belonging to the Union Tank Car line for hauling oil from Chama to their Alamosa refinery. Sixteen of these were shipped to the White Pass & Yukon later that year, though several of these have now been returned to Chama, while another one is at the B.C. Forest Museum. Also still on the D&RGW roster were 22 narrow gauge steam locomotives, 11 cabooses, 12 passenger cars and a variety of non-revenue equipment including the two rotary plows, flangers, pile driver, derrick and many outfit cars.

(Opposite below) The other end of the car shop, looking towards the roundhouse, in July 1965. Sign over the doorway says, "Engines not permitted through car shed." The crews in here had their work cut out trying to keep the antique rolling stock together. The building was torn down a few years later.

(Right) Just in from Chama, No. 484 rides the Durango turntable while No. 464 rests in the background. The three workmen show us why this is called an "Armstrong" turntable.

Both pages: AHW photos

Durango Yard Scenes
May 1962

(Left) A long line of spare narrow gauge wheels occupies this track by the sand house, while Nos. 480 and 488 steam patiently nearby, in between freight runs.

(Above left) The depot parking lot holds an interesting assortment of vehicles, including Fred Hust's blue '59 Buick that brought us on this trip to the narrow gauge.

(Above) Back side of the coal tower, showing the raised track where gondolas brought in the fuel.

(Next page, left) Front side of the coal tower, showing the chute which filled up locomotive tenders. Further back is the double-spouted water tank. The tank was removed in 1966 and tipple in 1967.

(Upper right) Early morning light bathes Mikado No. 488 as a hostler prepares her for another freight trip.

(Lower right) An empty gondola waits by the ash pit for the next locomotives to be cleaned out, while boxcars line both tracks by the car shed for running repairs.

Both pages, AHW photos

Tribute to the *Old* Durango Roundhouse

One of North America's last original working steam roundhouses was built in 1881 with ten stalls, then later reduced to six. In 1971 four stalls were added back on, but sadly, in February 1988 the whole building met its fiery end. Thus, the scenes in these photos no longer exist. Instead, there is a brand new roundhouse here, bigger and even better. We should be seeing plenty more photos similar to these in times to come. By now the place has an atmosphere much deeper than just the buildings, the company name, or even the old train equipment. It is the combined spirit of the many railroaders whose lives were focused here over the past century.

(Left) Inside the old Durango roundhouse back when its engines still hauled freight as well as passengers. No. 478 was sitting out the Silverton run, scheduled for a boiler wash, while No. 484 is called for a trip to Farmington with some boxcars the next morning. A portable radio nearby allows Bob Dylan to serenade these two with his 1965 comment, "Like a Rolling Stone."

(Below) On the same day, motor car MW02 rests further back in the roundhouse, representing one of the latest in an interesting series of motorized rail vehicles that have called on Durango. Custom built by Fairmont for the D&RGW, it was used by officials to inspect the line. The first known picture of this unique machine shows it behind the last northbound train on the Chili line out of Santa Fe. Changed, wrecked and rebuilt several times, it now sits in the enginehouse at Chama sporting a yellow paint job and a '48 Merc flathead under the hood.
Both photos, AHW

(Opposite) A night-time drama at the Durango roundhouse around 1960; stalls full of hefty steam locomotives fired up and ready for the call to work. Shown are Nos. 497, 487 and 484, plus motor car MW02 in the background. The photographer, a long time Santa Fe employee, ended up spending his final working years at the railroad in Durango.
Andy Saez Photo

Some Unusual Motive Power in Durango

(Top left) Rio Grande Southern Motor No. 4 represents the first serious inroad on steam powered railroading in this part of the world. Nicknamed the "Galloping Geese," a fleet of these three-foot gauge bus and boxcar mongrels started hauling the U.S. mail and some passengers between Durango, Mancos, Dolores, Rico and Ridgeway in the 1930s. In this scene, No. 4's cab door stand open and waiting at Durango in July 1939. A couple of passengers are already getting themselves settled into the back seat for a bouncing ride, while an old mechanic with bucket and toolbox inspects the unit's running gear.

(Bottom left) A more serious threat to steam power in the narrow gauge capital was this homely refugee from the U.S. Army, trying out as a helper on the Silverton train in May 1954. No. 4700N (for narrow gauge) was one of two experimental diesels brought by the Army, along with some rolling stock, for performance tests on the D&RGW between Alamosa, Durango and Farmington. Reports say the diesels were no match for steam, though the viewers may have been biased. At any rate, the diesels left after a season or two, while steam remains. Both, Railway Negative Exchange/AHW collection

(Opposite) Motorized power came to Durango once again in the mid-1960s with the arrival of little four-wheeled switcher No. 50. Of greater vintage than one might think, this unit began life on the wood-burning Sumpter Valley Railroad of Oregon as No. 101, back in 1937. At Durango it replaced recently retired 2-8-2 No. 464 in preparing the daily Silverton trains and doing some light freight switching around town. On this hot July afternoon in 1965, No. 50 is hauling boxcar 3705 and a string of flats up from a remnant of the former Rio Grande Southern mainline. These cars left for Alamosa behind steam the next day. AHW photo

(Above) No doubt one of the most luxurious observation platforms on the narrow gauge lines today - as it has been for over 100 years, - is the ornate private car "Nomad." Built as a chair car by Billmeyer and Small of Pennnsylvania in 1878, it became business car "N" after a rebuilding in 1886 by D&RG shop crews. Among the dignitaries who have held on to these brass railings were two U.S. presidents, Theodore Roosevelt and Ulysses Grant. The car was exhibited at the St. Louis World's Fair in 1904, the San Francisco Fair of 1915 and at Chicago's Century of Progress in 1933. In 1949 it was temporarily named the "General Wm. J. Palmer" during a visit to the Chicago Railroad Fair, in company with the other car on this page. Owned by several private parties beginning in 1951, the car fortunately remained on the railroad and was bought back by the D&SNG in 1982.

(Above left) A retired admiral and his wife had chartered the "Nomad" on this summer day in 1965 for the cost of $200, which included an attendant, though the fee is now at least five times that much. The scene is along the Animas River near the edge of Durango, with a state fish hatchery pond lying calmly next to the tracks. Both, AHW photos

(Left) The "David Moffat" was a forerunner of covered tourist cars still in use out of Durango and Chama today. It was built in 1949 to haul tourists on the imaginary "Cripple Creek and Tincup RR" at the Chicago Railroad Fair. Here, the car is seen back home in Durango during 1951 in between trips to Silverton. It later went to the Black Hills Central RR in South Dakota, then was sold to the operators of a tourist railroad at Central City, Colorado. AHW collection

"Silver Vista"
The Narrow Gauge Dome Car

The Rio Grande's Silverton branch enjoyed an upswing of passenger traffic after World War II as tourists and travellers learned about it. To make the trip more memorable, shop forces in Alamosa built this one-of-a-kind narrow gauge dome car, the "Silver Vista." From its lowly status as work train coach No. 313, it became the observation post of choice for those travelling up and down Animas Canyon for fun and with cameras. Built in 1948, the car unfortunately had a short life, destroyed in a car shop fire at Alamosa in September 1953.

(Above) The "Silver Vista" is shown backing into Silverton in July 1951, hand signals being relayed up to the head-end from this rear brakeman on his high perch.

(Above right) Aboard the "Silver Vista," an intimate solarium rolling on narrow gauge wheels through incredible scenery. Just one of the many ways this route has been enjoyed.

(Below, right) Happy faces, riding the narrow gauge in those carefree days after the big war. The crowd is enjoying the scenery and smiling for the photographer while up ahead the engine has stopped for water at the Needleton tank.
Three photos, AHW Collection

Durango to Silverton
In the Cab with John Coker

"After meeting the crew in the Durango roundhouse at call time and signing in, you walk with your fireman down to the assigned engine parked by the coal dock to the west, while the rest of the men go out to inspect the train. By the time you've finished oiling around, one of the brakemen shows up to switch your engine on the train. On the way there, you cross Sixth Street in a swirl of steam and smoke, as the shutters of visiting photographers click.

"After your train is assembled you perform the customary brake test while parked in front of the depot. Passengers begin to board, while ranchers and backpackers load their provisions into a boxcar at the head end, which is what continues to make this a mixed train. While you wait for the conductor to come up with the train orders, you enjoy your last cigarette and cup of coffee before getting down to serious work. This can be an enjoyable moment of respite, especially if the conductor is an old friend with whom you can enjoy a few laughs.

"The conductor compares his watch with yours, then heads back to the train while your fireman starts building a head of steam. Several tourists are probably hanging around near the engine at this point, eager to catch your attention and ask a few questions, which you answer patiently. Perhaps one will even try to get a ride up in the cab, but this is strictly forbidden. Incidentally, that policy is mainly because of insurance considerations which came about after a 1950s Rio Grande standard gauge boiler explosion, in which the crew and two unauthorized cab riders were killed.

"Eventually the conductor calls "all aboard" and gives you a highball, which is your signal to get the train underway. As it starts rolling, you blow the whistle repeatedly, holding down your speed and watching the many road crossings in this busy mountain town. Within minutes you'll be rolling through the wide Animas Valley, with its hayfields, orchards and homes, enjoying the friendship of local folks waving from back porches, tractors and gardens. Flocks of ducks and other wildlife are commonly seen from here on.

"At this point the trip is still fairly leisurely, with even the fireman having a chance to sit for a spell and enjoy the morning. After passing the first water tank, at Hermosa, the climb begins with a 2 1/2% grade. Soon the tracks rise above the valley floor, giving everyone on the train the first glimpse of high mountain ranges that lie ahead. The fireman is shovelling steadily now, as we enter a shady gap and cross a mountain brook, blowing our whistle as we enter the old stage stop of Rockwood, a very scenic place. Rockwood Cut signifies the entrance to the spectacular Animas Canyon, which we'll follow clear to Silverton.

"Our first stop is a few miles beyond the gorge at Ah! Wilderness dude ranch, where provisions and a few passengers are usually unloaded. A bit of old-time railroading flavour comes alive here each day at train time, with the folks who work and live at this isolated ranch taking a break to pick up their supplies and greet new guests arriving on the only link to the outside world.

"We stop to take on water for the first time at Tank Creek. As the fireman pulls the spout down to the tender, you climb down with your long stemmed oil can in hand and lubricate the locomotive's running gear.

"Now rolling along directly beneath the high peaks of the Grenadier Range, we traverse grassy meadows and groves of aspen where we may catch a glimpse of elk, or a black bear foraging for berries and roots. Sometimes these animals will run at the train's approach, other times they'll stand their ground and let the cars roll past them.

"At Needleton we usually make a brief stop to let off backpackers who want to hike in this wild country, after which we pull ahead a short distance to the wooden tank for more water. Virtually all the track in this area has been washed out at one time or another by the Animas River flooding from storms. Another concern from here to Silverton are the many avalanche paths that can suddenly block the line with snow, rock and trees.

"A short, steep climb brings us to one of the most majestic locations on the narrow gauge - Elk Park - where Mount Garfield dominates. After this tranquil interlude we start the final leg of our journey to Silverton by entering a narrow, rugged, boulder strewn stretch of canyon where we keep a sharp eye out for rocks on the track. Spectacular waterfalls and rushing mountain streams are on all sides, coming down the incredibly steep mountain slopes. For a moment or two you dwell on the determination of men with dreams of fortune who mined this remote land and built the railroad.

"Suddenly the narrow canyon opens up into 'Baker's Park' where the shiny metal roofs of Silverton catch your eye and signify that the climb is almost over. All that's left is to pass the old wooden station and come to a stop at Blair Street in the heart of town. After a two hour layover, you'll head back down to Durango, which is easier, your main challenge being to properly handle the braking in order to get the train and passengers home safely."

(Opposite) Section 2 of "the Silverton" waits impatiently as Section 1 blasts out of Durango behind No. 476.
AHW photo
(Above) "My good friend Shawn, a fellow railroader on the Colorado Narrow Gauge."
Watercolour by John Coker

The Silverton Branch

(Right) "Blasting upgrade towards Silverton," as seen and photographed by my 10 year old son Okan one early fall morning in 1983. It is a timeless scene, much like another that I took myself as a teenager. How many years before was the first time No. 473 stopped for water here at the Hermosa tank? Behind the narrow gauge Mikado rolls a string of bright coaches, the midst of them humping over the 64-foot wooden pony Howe-truss bridge that spans Hermosa Creek. We're in the Rockies at over six thousand feet, which is in itself a grand drama; but for the moment, this father and son team are mesmerized by the conveyance that's thundering by. And what thoughts among all those who are riding inside?
Okan Hungry Wolf photo

(Left) Even if the narrow gauge tracks no longer went to Silverton and this is all that was left around the yard, there'd be people coming from far and wide to see it. Many changes have been made in recent years, yet this 1983 photo is proof that the essence of Colorado narrow gauge railroading remains alive and well here. Makes you wonder if a brakeman will climb up this boxcar later on to release the brakewheel so a freight can take it away.....
AHW photo

(Left) Here's one of the classic spots for photographing the Silverton train, when it stops for water at the Needleton tank. Although No. 478 has undergone a face lift since this May 29, 1960 photo, scenes like this still take place on many days.
R.H. Kindig photo

(Below left) Here's No. 476 working upgrade across an old hand-built stone retaining wall. The engine is back to wearing a more traditional style stack during the fall of 1989. The train carried private car "Nomad" on this trip, chartered by a small party seeking the ultimate in a luxury ride through Animas Canyon. On a different scale, you can also charter liveable boxcars for the ride, then get parked along the way.
Okan Hungry Wolf photo

Buster Keaton
on the Silverton

(Above) Can you tell which one is the sad-faced comedian? He was dressed as conductor for a part in the Nat Holt film "DENVER & RIO GRANDE," being made along the Silverton line in the summer of 1947. Standing with him in more workaday conductor's duds is Myron Henry, a well known regular on this branch for many years. The Paramount production featured a head-on collision between two trains that cost over $150,000 to film and, unfortunately, destroyed all the equipment including two antique engines. Some 50 of the oldest cars left on the narrow gauge system were rounded up for use in this film, along with still preserved 2-8-0 No. 268, which was ferried down from her home in Gunnison, 300 miles to Alamosa aboard a standard gauge flatcar, running on her own power from there to the film site past Durango.
R.H. Kindig Collection

(Right) Headed back to Durango in May 1962, the classic "Silverton Train" passes one scenic spectacle after another.
AHW photo

Animas Canyon

(Opposite) Says the photographer: *"The 'High Line' on the Silverton Branch was a favorite place to attempt photography. It involved a walk down the track from Rockwood for a mile or so, to reach the area where the tracks wind along a cliff several hundred feet above the river. Old advertising and news stories exaggerated the distance sometimes to as much as 1,500 feet. The movie people loved this area to use in their Westerns. Until the last big mine closed in Feb. 1953, the branch ran mixed trains about once a week in winter. Though, when weather was bad no train might run for several weeks if not longer. Snow was not a problem on the lower third or half of the line, as Durango and the wide valley for a few miles north received little snow and drifts were rarely a concern. But the northern half of the line and Silverton might receive up to several feet of snow, which drifted badly in the canyon due to constant wind. There were a number of places where slides ran during the winter, so a couple engines of the K27 Class 2-8-2 would use a huge headlight-high wedge plow instead of normal pilot.*
"Here is 463 on such a trip, having encountered no snow in the first 15 miles of the branch, winding along the High Line where in 1882 the right of way was blasted with black powder tamped into drill holes by men lowered on ropes from above. If a deep or extensive slide were encountered, the engine would be uncoupled and hit the slide at about 20-25 miles an hour, after section men had probed it to be sure the snow didn't include any dangerously large rocks. If rocks were encountered, those would be dynamited. After plowing through a slide, the engine would then couple up and trip be resumed. This often meant a long round trip, train perhaps not getting back to Durango until midnight or later. One cause of delay was lack of a coupler on the big plow, necessitating plowing up to cars at Silverton, then engine wyeing, so it could back to the cars and couple in doing switching."
Robert W. Richardson photo

(Above) Passengers on the Silverton Mixed were often invited to ride in the cupola of the caboose, which gave them this kind of view. The conductor usually brewed up a big pot of coffee a For countless people riding the train to Silverton remains the trip of a lifetime. This scene shows engine 478 on Train #462, near Cascade Tank on July 1, 1939. Revenue freight includes the tank car, just ahead, plus reefer, boxcars and stock cars.
Paterson-George collection

(Right) One of the greatest challenges to narrow gauge railroad building in Colorado was right here in the significantly named Rio de los Animas - River of Lost Souls. Known as the "High Line," this section was blasted out of steep red granite walls hundreds of feet above the river in 1882 at the astronomical cost of $100,000 a mile. For passengers, this century-old pass is a highlight marked by slow speed, squealing flanges, groaning cars and spectacular vistas down into the abode of the souls.
Johnny Krause photo

Silverton

(Above) K-28 No. 463 was for many years one of the regular engines on the Silverton Mixed Train, as seen here on July 15, 1947 near the depot.
Fred Hust photo

(Right) As the consist of the Silverton Mixed grew, engines of the 470 class became the preferred power. Here is No. 473 in the Rio Grande gold paint scheme used during the early 1950s backing to the depot with five freight cars, a caboose, four coaches and observation car "Silver Vista."
Fred Hust photo

(Below) Sister engine 476 rolls down the same stretch of track some 30 years later, now on the Durango & Silverton, with relatively little having changed in the way of atmosphere.
Adolf and Okan Hungry Wolf photo

A Modern-Day Narrow Gauge Vacation

For over 100 years, train travellers arriving in Durango have enjoyed luxurious rooms at the Strater Hotel, near the depot. Its antique decor continues to set the mood for many heading to Silverton aboard D&SNG RR coaches, parlour cars or private cars. In Silverton, the Victorian-age Grand Imperial Hotel also offers antique rooms for those wanting a truly memorable two-day narrow gauge excursion.

(Right) Getting off the train in Silverton is like stepping into a western movie set - except that everything is for real. If you stay here at the Grand Imperial, you can watch the day's trains leave, knowing that your own won't go until tomorrow.

(Below) Antique luxury travel! At right stands D&SNG No. 350, the parlour car "Alamosa," which you can ride for extra fare. It was built in 1880 by famous car makers Jackson & Sharp as chair car No. 25, the "Hidalgo." In 1919 it was rebuilt into a private office and living car, after which it became a parlour-smoker. In 1937 it was rebuilt again as parlour-buffet car "Alamosa" for service on the "San Juan Express." When that train ended, the car became a coach on the "Silverton," losing its kitchen buffet and gaining steel siding. Finally in 1981, D&SNG crews rebuilt the parlour interior to carry 28 passengers. At left, the red-painted "Cinco Animas" is one of three plush private cars available for charter on the D&SNG RR. Built by D&RG in 1883 as sleeper No. 103, rebuilt several times, then sold privately to Oklahoma in 1954, it was brought back to Durango in 1963 by five ambitious individuals for whom the car is now named the "Cinco Animas," or "Five Souls."

Both AHW photos

Men, Machines and Mountains

SILVERTON

(Left) Not a whole lot has changed about this scene over the past 100 years or so, since men started driving steam locomotives up here into Silverton. There's not many towns left that survive principally as old time steam train destinations, the way Silverton does. Its Grand Imperial Hotel was completed in 1883 mainly to serve arriving train passengers, who continue to enjoy some of its original Victorian charm. Where else can you go by narrow gauge train, stay in a century-old hotel, taking the train back another day? Durango and Silverton enginemen Denny Shilthuis (left) and John Coker are seen here in the autumn of 1989 discussing the upgrade trip they had just finished.

(Opposite) There's a relaxed atmosphere in Silverton even when two full train loads of tourists have arrived. The immediate grandeur of surrounding mountains makes everything else seem rather insignificant. It also makes this pair of trains more of a teamwork operation, bringing people here just for the experience.
Both, AHW photos

Galloping Goose Portraits

Among the most distinct and unlikely fleets of narrow gauge equipment were the Rio Grande Southern's Galloping Geese, which not only developed a loyal group of fans but even managed to survive relatively intact, if somewhat scattered, into these modern times.

Conceived during the Depression, the Geese are credited with keeping the RGS going into the 1950s when logically it should have been pulled up a decade or two earlier. They provided service through the 30s and 40s whenever traffic was not enough to support full trains and crews, at the very least fulfilling the railroad's mail delivery contracts and providing passengers with very memorable rides.

(Below) Goose No. 1 was smaller than the rest of the flock and did not stay in service long, but No. 2 (officially called Motor No. 2) principally a freight hauler with a spare back seat for passengers, continues to see occasional service at the Colorado Railroad Museum in Golden. This August 1947 portrait shows the bus outside the roundhouse at Ridgeway.
Railway Negative Exchange/AWH Collection

(Right) A recent view from the back seat of Motor No. 2, looking downhill towards a work car and its volunteer crew at the Colorado Railroad Museum.
A&OHW photo

Three Incarnations of Galloping Goose No. 4

(Above) In this January 1939 portrait at Durango, RGS Motor No. 4 has just arrived in the fresh snow. Note that this is a three-truck Goose, longer than two-truck No. 2. The main body is a 1920 Pierce-Arrow, the box was custom built by RGS crews, and power came from a brand new Ford V-8 engine.
Railway Negative Exchange/AHW Collection

(Below) Sporting a newer bus body, though still with the original basic hood and freight box, No. 4 is seen on July 13, 1949 during a brief stop at Dallas Divide.
John Lawson Photo/W.C. Whittaker Collection

(Below left) Here's Motor No. 4 at the Ridgeway depot on September 1, 1951 in its final configuration, with the box rebuilt for passengers - mostly tourists who provided the line's main business in its final seasons. Proudly displaying its nickname and logo, the unit also lists some of its scenic destinations, including Ophir Loop, Lizard Head, Thompson Park and the Dores Canyon. Since retirement, it has been parked in Telluride.
Railway Negative Exchange/AHW Photo

(Left) Does this remind you of looking down at somebody's model railroad? Within the tight confines around the Rio Grande Southern's station at Ophir, Colo. some unrecorded traveller got this close-up view of Galloping Goose No. 4 in its second-to-last configuration. It must be a hot sunny day; the gentleman on the station platform has his jacket underarm and more notably, the Goose has both sides of her hood propped partly open. The steep rugged area around Ophir was considered by many to be a highlight on the whole fabulous Narrow Gauge Circle. Imagine how this silver beast had to struggle at times to get over those high mountain grades on hot, windy days.

AHW collection

(Opposite) Stepping lightly across Lightener Creek trestle, Galloping Goose No. 5 has just left Durango headed westbound on the Rio Grande Southern. This was the final configuration for the Geese, after mail service ended and the boxcar section was opened to carry passengers. These can be considered American folk art of the transportation sector. Amazingly, over the years only a few of them were wrecked - usually by derailing at speed after a loss of brakes on steep downgrades - and there were no recorded fatalities.

Johnny Krause photo

COKER
5-92

Montrose, Colorado
Two of These Three Survived

(Above) Only a dirty mound of snow at the left indicates that this is actually a cold January day in 1953, outside the D&RGW two-stall enginehouse at Montrose, Colorado. Proud little 2-8-0 No. 318 lost her job not too long after this, but she was saved by Bob Richardson. 2-8-2 No. 454 wasn't quite so lucky, being turned into scrap instead.
Railway Negative Exchange/AHW Collection

(Opposite top) A warm September afternoon in 1951 finds ill-fated No. 454 at the Montrose enginehouse, while on a nearby siding sits a pair of Consolidations led by No 340, soon to become Knott's Berry Farm No. 40. A fourth engine is parked inside. Note that all trackage is dual gauge.
Railway Negative Exchange/AHW Collection

(Opposite bottom) Here's No. 318 almost forty years later, stripped down at the Colorado Railroad Museum in Golden, where she's expected to be under steam again. The setting here reminds one of a scale modeller's intricate diorama - with a myriad of engines, cars, parts, buildings and trackwork - but all in real size. The combined collection is a treasure trove of Colorado narrow gauge railroading, alive and outdoors, like a living history book.
AHW Photo

Gunnison, Colorado

(Above) Rods down and counterbalances up, outside-framed 2-8-0 No. 361 stands in front of the Gunnison depot flying the white flags of an extra. With baggage car, four coaches and an open gondola on the rear, this train has just returned from one of the last excursion trips through the famed Black Canyon of the Gunnison, on September 7, 1947. Railway Negative Exchange/AHW Collection

(Below) Looking from the coal tower at Gunnison, we see 2-8-0 No. 268 taking water, while nearby are parked homemade spreader OV (very left), caboose 0588, plus some outfit cars. At one time this was an important terminal for two narrow gauge railroads, the D&RG and the DSP&P. Johnny Krause photo

Farewell Trip
Through the Black Canyon

(Above) In May 1949 the Rocky Mountain Railroad Club sponsored the last scheduled trip from Gunnison to Cimarron and return, going through the winding, cavernous Black Canyon of the Gunnison along the way. This was the Denver & Rio Grande's original transcontinental route from Denver to Utah, though by the 1940s it had long been relegated to secondary status. Powering the final excursion was 2-8-0 No. 361, seen here being turned on the wye at Cimarron as fans wander around seeking photo angles. The line actually went on to Montrose, but the train turned back here since the fans had come mainly to experience the legendary canyon. The old conductor riding the pilot has dressed in his finest for the occasion, as he guides the engine across U.S. highway 50. In the background can be seen Cimarron's water tank, section house, a small bridge and pump house.
Photo: A.M. Payne Collection/from John Coker

(Right) Later that afternoon No. 361 and its sizable train stop for the final time at famous Currecanti Needle, a rock pinnacle in the Black Canyon of the Gunnison. For many years the image of Currencanti Needle was in the centre of the herald used by the Denver & Rio Grande on virtually all its advertising, stationary, crockery and silverware. The tip of the needle now looks down on a reservoir that has flooded this spot.
Photo: John Coker collection

The Baldwin Branch

(Above) D&RGW C-16 No. 278 sits near the Gunnison roundhouse on this sunny July 4th morning in 1940, ready to go out as helper on the Baldwin branch.

(Above left) A little later the same day we see No. 223 working upgrade with three boxcars and a string of coal empties destined for the mine at the end of the Baldwin branch.

(Left) At the back of the same train is older No. 278, pushing against the caboose. Of special note is the fact that both of these handsome 2-8-0s still survive. No. 223 went on display at Salt Lake City the year after these pictures were taken, while No. 278 now belongs to the U.S. Park Service and is on display on an old D&RG bridge at the mouth of the Black Canyon of the Gunnison, coupled to a boxcar and caboose 0577.

Three photos by Jackson Those/John Coker Collection

Marshall Pass

(Right) Railroad tracks winding upgrade as far as the eye can see in this 1880's mounted portrait taken up on Marshall Pass between Gunnison and Salida. This was then the mainline from Denver to Salt Lake City. Consolidation No. 41 looks shiny and new, but there's more folks around her than just those in the crew - among them are three ladies! Their reasons for being there would surely make an interesting account.
AHW collection

(Below) Marshall Pass again, this time on May 2, 1955, showing D&RGW 2-8-2 No. 483 taking water at Mears Jct. for the very last trip over this spectacular piece of railroad. Helper engine No. 489 waits its turn in the background. These engines were ferried south to Alamosa by standard gauge cars after this line closed. No. 483 now works out of Chama.
R.H. Kindig photo

MARSHALL PASS.

The Monarch Branch

(Above) A double switchback was built in 1883 to bring this branchline from Salida up to gold and silver mines that gave out before these pictures were taken in 1952. No. 489 is leading a string of empty gondolas up to be filled with high quality limestone, which will be transferred to standard gauge cars at Salida for shipment to the steel mills near Pueblo.

(Left) No. 485 is the helper, though even with two engines the typical empty train of 50-some cars had to be taken upgrade in two sections. Caboose 0574 was built in 1886 and is today still in service.
Both photos, Railway Negative Exchange/AHW Collection

Here's a glimpse of a famous engine in the Denver & Rio Grande yard at Salida back in February 1908. Most early day photos of Colorado railroading have been published, especially those showing locomotives that still exist. This rare, though somewhat scratched negative turned up in the pages of an old book. Equipped with wide footboards and three couplers for dual gauge switching, C-16 class 2-8-0 No. 268 was already near 30 years old here. She spent many years working out of Salida, often making trips to Gunnison, Crested Butte and Cimarron. In the 1930s the engine was transferred to Durango, working as yard switcher and as occasional road engine on the RGS. After 1940 she was sent back to the Gunnnison area, mostly working the Baldwin branch. In 1947 she starred in the Paramount movie "Denver & Rio Grande" and in 1949 she went to the Chicago Railroad Fair. No. 268 is now on display at Gunnison, Colorado.
AHW Collection

Rio Grande Cabooses

According to D&RGW freight car expert Robert E. Sloan, the railroad used some 121 narrow gauge cabooses over the years, consisting primarily of five different types along with a few unique cars. Short four-wheeled cabooses were the earliest type, 68 of these having been built between 1871 and 1881, most in the D&RG shops at Denver and Alamosa. The only survivor from this bunch is on display in Silverton.

(Above left) Caboose 0500 was built in 1886 as the road's second No. 1, a short 17 foot car with eight wheels instead of four. It became No. 0500 during a general renumbering in 1887. Seen here at Durango in July 1941, the car was sold in 1950 to Bob Richardson for his Narrow Gauge Motel in Alamosa, where it is still on display.

(Below left) "Conductor of Extra East, waiting for his crew and engine to bring the rest of his train," says the note on this photo, taken in the Chama yard on May 9, 1951. Caboose 04343 was built in 1883 as a 24-foot boxcar! This was rebuilt in 1895 into a 30-foot boxcar and in 1897 as a work caboose. In 1914 it was rebuilt again as a regular caboose. Since the end of narrow gauge freight service, it has been stored in one of the surviving Alamosa roundhouse stalls.

(Above) The Silverton mixed train shows an interesting mix of passengers during this stop sometime in 1948, soon after tourists and railfans had discovered the line. Trailing caboose 0540 is a 30 foot car built by the D&RG in 1881 and rebuilt in 1923. It is still in service at Durango.
Three photos, Railway Negative Exchange/AHW collection

(Opposite) Second to last caboose built for D&RG narrow gauge service was No. 0588, new in December 1900, rebuilt in 1942, seen here somewhere near Salida in the early 1950s, with 2-8-2 No. 483 behind as helper. This caboose is now on display at Cimarron, Colorado.
Johnny Krause photo

Rio Grande Scenes
From the Camera of R.H. Kindig

(Left) Rio Grande Southern 4-6-0 No. 25 on the trestle below Durango on June 30, 1938.

(Lower left) D&RGW 2-8-2 No. 463 with Mixed Train #462 at Silverton, Colorado, Aug. 20, 1952. At this time freight traffic was still worthwhile and the passenger consist was growing.

(Below) A Rocky Mountain Railroad Club excursion of an earlier vintage was this one behind D&RGW 2-8-0 No. 361, crossing the Gunnison River in the Black Canyon on September 7, 1947. Parlor car "Chama" brings up the rear end. Today it still runs on the Knott's Berry Farm railroad.

(Opposite Page, right) The Rio Grande Southern's handsome 2-8-0 No. 42 is seen at the Ridgeway water tank on June 30, 1939. This C-17 is the only survivor of its class, now on the roster of the Durango and Silverton Narrow Gauge Railroad.

(Far right) Here's the back of No. 42 on one of Ridgeway's roundhouse tracks, parked beside 4-6-0 No. 22 and borrowed 2-8-2 No. 463, same day as above.

(Centre right) About a year later No. 42 is seen working hard, flying white flags, at the head of a 14 car extra in charge of 2-8-2 No. 455. The photographer notes that the train was near Peak, Colo., doing a mere 10 mph on Aug. 24, 1940.

All six photos, R.H. Kindig.

"Old Railroaders" - John Coker

• Samples From Bob Richardson's Photo Box •

(Above) April storms are not uncommon at Poncha Junction, as in this 1950 scene of No. 489 drifting in with a freight from Marshall Pass. Occasions like these test the real commitment some photographers make to record every facet of their subject's operations. Bob could have stayed by a heater at the motel and read a magazine instead, then we'd never know this moment.

(Left) How about "Narrow Gauge Archeology" for a semester course? Here's a crew skillfully dislodging what may at first seem to be a dinosaur bone but is in fact a diamond stack at a wreck site on the two foot gauge Gilpin Tramway in Colorado.

(Right) More archeology! What have we here, King Tut's tomb? No, it's one of three long abandoned tunnels of the Colorado Midland near Buena Vista. This photo is in tribute to that hardy branch of souls who likes to tramp the vacant roadbeds of disappeared railroads.

Photos on both pages, Robert W. Richardson

(Clockwise from top left)

1. "Cat escort, when taking pix," says Bob's note on the back of this snapshot, taken on a winter day at the famed Colorado Railroad Museum, which he founded years ago in Golden, Colorado. Restored 2-8-0 No. 346, Galloping Goose No. 2 and a few of the many rare pieces of rolling stock are in the background.

2. "Mr. Bradshaw's good deed: taking the 'goofy stacks' off the 473-476-478: Durango." Some 30 years of contrived "Wild West" look on the Silverton ended with this pile of scrap near the Durango roundhouse.

3. "I like people pictures," says Bob, in response to my request for 'human interest shots.' Taken on Cumbres Pass in recent years.

4. "Burning the Museum mortgage." There's Bob himself, gladly ending the museum's land debts with the fire from No. 346, an 1881 Baldwin 2-8-0.

5. "Putting the headlight on a DSP&P engine at the museum."

6. "Getting rotary ready at Antonito in 1949. 15 miles away the drifts were higher than it."

All photos on both pages, Robert W. Richardson

(Right) How's this for an exclusive train? Two brakemen ride, while the conductor signals that there's just a foot or so before making the joint, as leased engine D&RGW No. 461 couples a boxcar up to business car B-2, the "Edna," for a trip on Rio Grande Southern rails. The car had just been painted for an upcoming excursion.

(Below) Another leased engine, No. 464, is seen drifting northbound with an RGS freight along the San Miguel River valley between Vance Junction and Placerville. It is the fall of 1950, next to last year of the line. Upon arrival at Placerville, a helper engine will be waiting to cut in halfway back of the train, to assist up the 3% grade to Dallas Divide, before dropping down the 12 mile stretch into Ridgeway. Cattle were loaded in these cars at Lizard Head pass earlier in the day.

Both pages, R.W. Richardson photos

(Above) An Ohio Shay. Although Bob Richardson is mainly known for his many years of devotion to the Colorado narrow gauges, it wouldn't be like him to show a bunch of photos without including something from his home state of Ohio. The scene was on one of his very first fantrips, and could be titled, "Photo Run-by in 1937." He joined a group visiting the three foot gauge Kelly's Island Lime & Transport Company railroad at Marblehead, Ohio in October of that year, when - it is believed - the first-ever quadruple-headed fantrip took place. The crude home built car was this line's only "coach," with endwise benches for the quarry workers. Note that the little two-truck Shay lacks a number and other identification.

(Below left) Even the old timers can't resist "one more shot" at a place like Windy Point - in this case showing the final passenger movement from Alamosa to Durango in 1967, with two K-27s and 20 cars.

(Below centre) No. 484 wheels a load of pipe past the depot at Aztec, N.M. on one of the last train trips made over the Farmington Branch, November 1966.

(Below right) "Vandalism!" says the photographer, showing what happened to a car of coal in Alamosa after someone opened its bottom doors. Maybe it was the guy who got to shovel all that coal up, needing himself a job.

Some Snapshots From Lad Arend

(Left) While the name Lad. G. Arend will be familiar to many longtime readers of RAILROAD Magazine, for most this will be the first look at one of the old timers in narrow gauge railfanning. No armchair buff was Lad, a true Boomer railroader who worked on lines all over the continent. He was killed at the age of 91 while driving his vintage sports car, still working as a conductor on the Strasburg Railroad. He wrote letters, traded pictures and rode on trains for fun whenever he wasn't working on them.

His love for the narrow gauge was consumated nearly every summer with a pilgrimage to Colorado. Being a railroader, he hung around more on the trains and with the crews, taking many precious photos of different lines in their twilight years. In his later years he lived aboard a retired interurban car in Ohio which he parked on its wheels under a big tree, then remodelled and named the "Chama." From then on, his frequent magazine ads offering photos for sale always included as part of the address, "Write to Car Chama." (Says Bob Sandusky: "He'd send me a dozen 5 x 7's for $1")

In this photograph, taken by someone else but with his own camera, we see Mr. Arend on the Rio Grande Southern at Vance Jct. in 1950. The print doesn't say whether he was just here to ride and take pictures, or if he was actually part of the crew; he sure looks as authentic as the Galloping Goose, or as the connecting highway truck behind him.

(Lower left) Here's a different Goose, "No. 3 unloading mail" somewhere out on the line, according to the note with this shot. We can assume Lad Arend got back inside before those doors were closed.

(Below) At Dolores, the RGS roadmaster poses with his converted railtruck, Motor No. 6, also known as the "Work Goose." With white flags indicating it was about to run extra somewhere, it's a good bet they brought the old visiting railroader along.

(Right) What's this, every narrow gauge fan's day dream of a private excursion from Durango to Silverton? "How many photo stops would you like, sir?" Actually, old No. 319 (built in 1895) was just the Durango yard switcher, probably making up the next day's "San Juan." She started her long life on the Florence & Cripple Creek Railroad up near Denver.

Now, getting back to that daydream - count me in line for the first chance to ride the "Nomad" behind No. 42 through Elk Park, as soon as she becomes available. I'd sure put a colour picture of that on the cover of a book!

(Centre) A boomer engine, as photographed by a boomer railroader. Obviously a little gathering of friends, the whole crew of five has posed with Rio Grande Southern 2-8-0 No. 74, standing in the yard at Durango in 1950. The engine began life as Colorado & Northwestern No. 30, then went to the Denver, Boulder & Western, followed by the Colorado & Southern, before completing her distinguished career on the RGS. She is now on display at Boulder, Colorado along with a coach and caboose.

(Left) The Colorado & Southern was the last railroad operating narrow gauge trains out of Denver, or any other large city in the U.S. Running over tracks that originally belonged to the legendary Denver, South Park & Pacific, the C&S had a variety of light motive power whose cinder-catching "beartrap" stacks appear to be an "acquired taste" in the way of railroad studies. Here's No. 68 and 58, both so equipped, ready to help push a freight train out of Denver and into the mountains during the final years before this part of narrow gauge railroading ended in 1937. We'll leave you to imagine what might have been up at the head end of this train. A four-wheeled caboose is bringing up the rear.

Photos on both pages by Lad G. Arend/Robert J. Sandusky Collection

Moments of Grandeur for an Otherwise Sad Train on the Colorado & Southern

(Above) The powers of nature are often strongly portrayed in pictures of narrow gauge railroading, as in this view of C&S 2-8-0 No 69 at Clear Creek Canyon, near Fall River, Colorado. Imagine the battles over the decades to keep tracks in a place like this from being covered by those eroding rocky mountains. Behind the engine comes 4-wheeled caboose No. 1006, followed by a little string of cars out on a final mission - carrying the rails that workmen are tearing up from behind. This was the last train to challenge that massive rock, March 1939. Caboose 1006 has survived and is on display at Silver Plume.

(Opposite page) Two years later, on May 10, 1941, No. 69 was recorded at Idaho Springs, Colorado with another final train; again work crews are loading up the rails as they get torn up from here in passing. Note the partially removed track in foreground. Although the railroad and the mining complex in back are both just memories, that imposing stone structure of the Idaho Springs Machine Works is still standing and in contemporary use. The old wooden miner's homes in the other scene at Idaho Springs are now about as scarce as old miners.

All three photos, RNE/AHW Collection

Georgetown Loop

(Above) A three car freight train recreates scenes of the past at one of narrow gauge railroading's most famous landmarks, the Georgetown Loop, west of Denver. Back in the late 1800s the 8 1/2 mile Georgetown, Breckenridge & Leadville Railroad first began to attract public attention with tracks that went up the canyon of Clear Creek and then passed over themselves on the Devil's Gate Viaduct, 300 feet long and almost 100 feet high. Later taken over by the Union Pacific, this short narrow gauge line sometimes saw half dozen or more tourist trains a day in addition to its two regular ones. Automobiles and trucks eventually lured the traffic away, so that the line was shut down and the famous bridge dismantled in 1939. One hundred years after the original was completed in 1884, a new version was dedicated for modern tourist traffic and for occasional freight scenes like this one. The engine is No. 40, a Baldwin 2-8-0 from the IRCA in El Salvador.

(Above left) Consolidation No. 40 waits in the siding while former West Side Lumber Company Shay No. 14 rattles by with its train of tourists. The three mile line is a project of the Colorado State Historical Society. Its engine roster includes sister Shays 8 and 12, plus sister Consolidation No. 44.

(Left) Signs of the past, at the Georgetown Loop Railroad's Silver Plume depot.
Three photos, Georgetown Loop Railroad

(Opposite) "The Loop - Union Pacific Ry. near Georgetown, Colorado," so says the fine print at the bottom of this old brown-toned photo card of the 1880s. That's the original bridge down below - same place where the one today brings trains similar to this. Back then it looked like a new model railroad layout - before putting in the scenery! As seen on the opposite page, the same place today is a tourist's delight and a popular destination. Note the dandies at the left, plus another train on the far-off hillsides. Would have been an interesting spot to sit for a busy day with a video camera! Lots of short trains.
W.H. Jackson photo/AHW collection

4. "THE LOOP."

W. H. JACKSON & CO.,
PHOTOGRAPHERS OF
ROCKY*MOUNTAIN*SCENERY
DENVER, COLORADO.

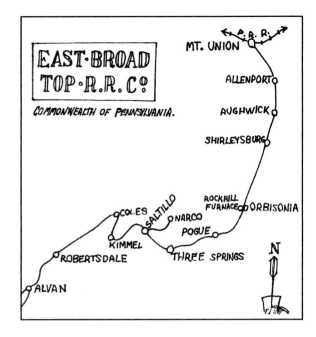

(Left above) Daily three-foot gauge railroading survived into the 1950s in Pennsylvania as seen here at the East Broad Top's Orbisonia station, where a message is about to be handed up to the crew of No. 17, ready to head out with some freight.
Johnny Krause photo

(Left below) Compare this scene with the one above, taken at nearly the same place some 30 years later. Although the track suggests a lack of upkeep, the strings of hoppers could have come in just last night, while the nearby freight office seems to be waiting for boxcars. This is the East Broad Top today.
AHW photo

(Opposite) Quick, which decade is this? The scene is almost timeless, though EBT experts will note details that were only added in recent years. The structure was built in 1903, the parlour car in the late 1800s. Both have been illustrated many times, so that a first visit here is likely to bring some dejavu.
AHW photo

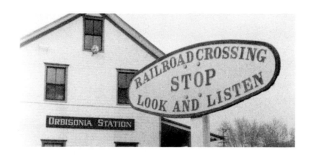

disturbed for a few years. Then, as part of a local celebration in 1960, he agreed to help some of the old timers get a train steamed up once again. Public response to the event was strong enough to keep the train going, thus beginning a new career for this historic railroad.

Since then, the East Broad Top's survival has become near legendary. "Winter Spectaculars" produced photos of double and tripleheaders in the snow. A lot of work was done with the original crews; even the operating vice president took his job back. Though only five miles of track was put to use, the highlight of the railroad was right around Orbisonia station. Of course, there's always talk about operating more mileage; several dozen miles of weed grown tracks remain unused, more or less in place. But even with no trains in sight that morning, it was easy to appreciate the East Broad Top's

East Broad Top Railroad

"Without doubt the East Broad Top has North America's best preserved steam railroad facility," declared Canadian rail historian Omer Lavallee during a visit in 1981, when I was headed from the Rockies to Pennsylvania. "There's no comparison to Durango," he added, though western narrow gauge fans would consider those fighting words. Out of respect I didn't ask if his opinion was partly eastern bias; he'd visited narrow gauge lines all over the world and spent much of his life with rail preservation work, so his statement carried considerable weight.

That Omer was right became apparent the moment I drove up to the EBT's Orbisonia depot one foggy morning soon after. Here was not just an original station and some tracks - though often that's the most on a railroad still left behind. Even the roundhouse nearby didn't really sum up the place - though precious few of those have been saved, especially with their original steam engines inside. Instead of one or two important rail structures, this place is a whole industrial neighborhood, including shops, warehouses and a freight yard full of old cars (not to mention the adjacent mining town of Rockhill Furnace) all of it looking as though it was shut down just for the weekend.

The place seemed deserted when I crunched to a halt in the parking lot and turned off my motor. By overlooking the car, it was hard to tell what decade suddenly had me surrounded. For a start, the two-story station seemed virtually the same as when I'd first seen it as a teenager, in 1950's magazines like *RAILROAD* and *Trains*. Described as one of railroading's "most recognizable corporate landmarks," I expected to see Johnny Krause or Phillip Hastings come around the corner with a 4x5 camera.

"Railroad Crossing," said a big oval sign nearby, "Stop, Look and Listen." It spoke to the people of another age, when there was more time to follow such sage advice. How many of today's visitors come there to contemplate these things, to stand back and truly stop, look and listen?

In front of this station runs North America's oldest narrow gauge railroad, chartered in 1856. It was also the last one operating east of the Mississippi, only closing down in 1956 when its lifeblood - the area's coal traffic - gave out. The East Broad Top's history could have ended there, with all the old stuff torn out, scrapped, or sold. In fact, in April of that year the whole railroad was indeed bought by the Kovalchick Salvage Company and few people really noticed.

Scrap dealers often capitalize on the demise of an operation like the EBT, but Nick Kovalchick was different from the rest. Realizing that he had control of something far greater than junk, he left the whole railroad sitting un-

(Above) More dejavu inside the station, at least on this special day in 1981. Seated downstairs at the desk is C. Roy Wilburn, operating vice president of the East Broad Top, both before its original demise and after its rebirth. He's discussing business with the boss, Joe Kovalchick, who took over as the railroad's president and owner after his father died in 1977. Instead of coal tonnage and schedules for hauling the mail, their trains now settle for the lighter cargo of short-haul passengers whose main interest is often to see the railroad's overall physical plant as a unique piece of history.
AHW photo

(Left) Way before tourists came around, EBT's No. 17 needed only a single combine to accommodate passengers, crew and express. This scene shows Train No 2 at Saltillo in August 1941, back when the EBT still scheduled three or four trains daily in each direction.
Railway Negative Exchange/AHW collection

(Opposite) Same engine, different era. Though No. 17 may only be hauling tourists these days, cleaning the old coal burner is still as hard and dirty as it was back in 1918 when it arrived new from Baldwin.
AHW photo

(Right) Early morning light filters through the fog and steam as East Broad Top No. 12 limbers up in the yard outside the roundhouse. It was the sound of this engine getting on the turntable that ended my station reverie on that first morning of my visit in 1981. This is a fitting "first shot" of EBT action, since it shows the road's oldest and lightest of six 2-8-2s, built by Baldwin in 1911. In all that time she's never known another railroad but this one. Building on right is the sandhouse, bell shaped object this side of there is top of water standpipe. Banjo switch stand is unique.
AHW photo

(Below) This time it's July 1949 and we're at Robertsdale, Pa., where no trains have run since 1956. On this occasion it's an excursion train, with Parlour Car No. 20 bringing up the rear end, as it still often does today. A real jewel of its type, the car once carried President Grover Cleveland.
Railway Negative Exchange/AHW collection

(Opposite, top right) Although this photo was taken in June 1932 (over 60 years ago) about the same scene still takes place on the yard tracks beyond Orbisonia station. Passenger service ended on the EBT some three years before the line's closure, yet a nice fleet of passenger cars has survived, most of them purchased second-hand from other narrow gauge lines in the early 1900s and thus of great historic value. Wooden No. 28 and sister 27 are the only two cabooses on the railroad.
C.E.S. photo/AHW collection

(Opposite, bottom right) Details of the narrow gauge car maker's art, with part of the roundhouse in the background.
AHW photo

(Opposite, left) Here's Caboose No. 28 on the day of my 1981 visit, trailing engine No. 12 and a short freight with several old cars that were originally built in the railroad's own shops. The culvert makes a simple project for narrow gauge model builders.
AHW photo

(Above) "Dinner Hour at Robertsdale" notes the photographer of this railfan special which ran over the EBT on September 17, 1950. White flags fly from the pilot, as is the line's custom. A number of fantrips were operated after the war, the standard cost being $60 for an engine and two coaches, up to 10 hours, with $30 more for each ten hours thereafter and $12 each for additional coaches. Excursions usually started out at Mt. Union on the north end of the line, where fans arrived aboard the standard gauge Pennsylvania Railroad. This train has six cars.
C.E.S. photo/AHW collection

(Above left) A regular passenger train ready to load some business into the single car at Mt. Union on April 27, 1940. In addition to a sizeable dual-gauge yard (where the EBT kept two standard gauge 0-6-0 switchers), Mt. Union was also the site of an important preparation plant, where coal brought from mines along the narrow gauge was cleaned and graded before heading out in standard gauge hoppers to other parts of the country. For some reason, the photographer has noted on this negative, "Ronald Miller, standing." Where are you now, my boy?
Railway Negative Exchange/AHW collection

(Below left) No. 15, about to run extra to Mt. Union with a load of coal, is seen here at Orbisonia on November 19, 1936, with white flags up and tender full.
Railway Negative Exchange/AHW collection

(Right) Forty-five years later, No. 15 rides the Armstrong turntable on her way to running some special trains for photographers. The big stone building in the background was an old farmhouse back in 1872 when the EBT bought all this land from T.E. Orbison, for whom the station and adjacent community are named. For railroad use it was turned into the Shop Superintendent's office.
AHW photo

(Left) One of the earliest fantrips on the East Broad Top was led by No. 14, back in May 1940, as seen here at the edge of Orbisonia. This engine was built in 1912, then stored for many years after the line shut down, until rebuilt for tourist service in 1987.
Railway Negative Exchange/AHW Collection

(Below) Last meet between two working freight trains on the East Broad Top was photographed March 23, 1956 in the snow along Sideling Hill. Extra 16 North trails 17 loads of coal and a coach (preferred over a caboose because of its smoother ride). These tracks lay idle today, as does No. 16 inside the Orbisonia roundhouse.
Johnny Krause photo

(Opposite) The ritual of helping stubborn coal flow faster down the chute and into the tender hasn't changed over the years, nor has the coaling facility itself, down at the south end of Orbisonia's yard, only now the stuff is brought from elsewhere by truck, instead of coming here from nearby mines by train.
AHW photo

(Left) While No. 17 waits to run extra with a short freight train, the crew of motor car M-1 gets ready to pick up passengers over at the depot. Coupled behind is coach No. 8, equipped with roller bearings many years ago for easier pulling, when this team still provided daily commuter service to miners living along the railroad.
AHW photo

(Below) Motor car M-1 stands ready for mail, express and a few passengers at Mt. Union in 1946. The 47-ton unit was bought as a "kit" from the Brill Co. in 1926, then assembled by EBT shop crews in Orbisonia. Powered by a 250-horsepower gas engine, it was able to pick up the occasional loaded freight car along the way, in addition to its own capacity for goods and passengers.
Railway Negative Exchange/AHW collection

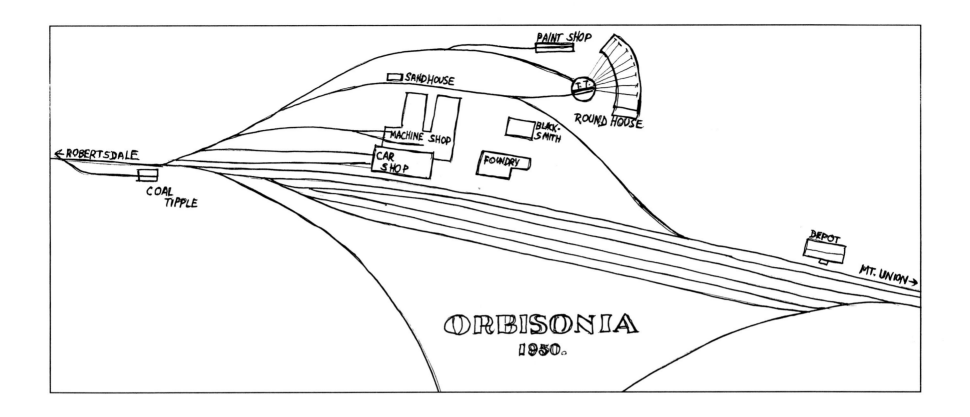

PAINT SHOP

SANDHOUSE

R.T.

ROUND HOUSE

MACHINE SHOP

BLACK-SMITH

CAR SHOP

FOUNDRY

←ROBERTSDALE

COAL TIPPLE

DEPOT

MT. UNION →

ORBISONIA

1950.

(Right) White flags signal an extra run south for 2-8-2 No. 16 as soon as she gets the caboose hooked on to her string of empties. Except that there's no more smoke coming out of the twin stacks at the shop complex today, Orbisonia yard still looks about the same as this early 1950s scene.
Johnny Krause photo

EAST BROAD TOP

(Left) Engine clean out time at the ashpit near the roundhouse and turntable sees a variety of tools used for reaching into the firebox and ashpan.
AHW photo

(Above) Another load of coal is ready to depart from Robertsdale behind No. 17 on this snowy March day in 1953.
Railway Negative Exchange/AHW collection

(Opposite) The same No. 17 is at the very right of this dramatic scene, behind No. 15 and adjacent to No. 12. Although the East Broad Top's five miles of serviceable track may offer only limited operations, the line can still come up with an occasional surprise. On this special 1981 weekend, the promised use of two engines turned into three when shop crews finished an overhaul ahead of schedule. In 1987 a promised three engines turned into the first recorded quadruple-header.
AHW photo

(Right above) A famous narrow gauge landmark was this interesting transfer crane built at Mt. Union in 1933 to lift up standard gauge cars, arriving on Pennsy tracks, so trucks could be switched fro trips over narrow gauge tracks. Although a crew of five men still took about half an hour per car for the work, this was less costly than reloading all the freight from standard to narrow gauge cars. NO 14 passes by with a passenger train in May 1940
Railway Negative Exchange/AHW collection

(Right below) Another passenger train passes the transfer crane about nine years later behind No. 16.
Railway Negative Exchange/AHW collection

(Opposite) The hostler watches his handiwork as No. 17 leaves her five sisters and backs out of the eight stall roundhouse. The first six stalls of this roundhouse were built in 1882, using brick and Pennsylvania fieldstone. Right after 1900 it was rebuilt, with two more stalls added for the expanding engine roster. Since the fire in Durango, this is North America's last original narrow gauge roundhouse.
AHW photo

(Opposite) Another example of the timeless feel that East Broad Top railroading continues to evoke. Crews stand by while No. 15 gets lined up for the grand event of 1981 - an unadvertised triple-header

(Right) Here's how the triple header looks from above as the fireman of the trailing engine checks out his fire.

(Far right) Bringing up the rear is red Caboose No. 28, appearing as neat and roadworthy as the day she was made. The scene is proof that it doesn't take much track to recreate the essence of vintage narrow gauge railroading. You can almost hear the whistles echoing from the hills of the serene Aughwick valley.
All three, AHW photos

Tweetsie

(Opposite, above) The motive power of a proud little carrier, East Tennessee and Western North Carolina Railroads No. 14 is as pretty as her company's name is long. This was one of five Baldwin-built Ten-wheelers on the line around the 1930s and 40s, all of them noted for their sporty appearances, attired in striking green, with gold lettering and striping, plus touches of scarlet and silver. Not bad for a hillbilly line remembered as "The Blue Ridge Stemwinder." This early morning portrait was taken outside the ET&WNC engine house at Johnson City, Tennessee in October 1946. Baldwin built No. 14 in 1917, the U.S. Army drafted it for service on the WP&Y, where it was damaged in the Skagway roundhouse fire and scrapped in 1945.

(Opposite below left) About halfway between the dual gauge yard at Johnson City (where the Tweetsie met the more famously green Southern Railway) and the other end of the line at Boone, there was Cranberry N.C., part of which is seen here in the early 1940s. This is about how an engineer on one of those Ten-wheelers would see the place on arriving to switch the cars. The Cranberry depot was reached by a spur from the mainline that switched back down a steep hillside.

(Opposite, below right) The Tweetsie ran a lot of picnic and baseball specials throughout its life, which probably explains the existence of open air tourist car No. 11, outfitted with passenger trucks and screened in benches. Built in 1911, the car still exists on today's version of the Tweetsie.

(Above right) Here's another of the Tweetsie's handsome Ten-wheelers, No. 11, leaking steam from its slide valves in this 1945 view. Five years later, in the spring of 1950, this engine pulled the line's last train, then was cut up for scrap. Only sister No. 12 survived, operating today on a nearby tourist line also called Tweetsie, based at Blowing Rock, N.C.
(Below left) Forest and mining products were the main traffic for Tweetsie trains, so the roster had a number of cars like this well made, drop bottom gondola No. 24, seen in typical hillbilly country.

(Below right) Tank cars like No. 604 were used to haul fuel to several customers along the ET&WNC. According to information stencilled on its side: "Tank Tested, Pressure 50 lbs. per squ. inch at Johnson City, Tenn. by E.T. &W. N.C. 8-39."
All photos, Railway Negative Exchange/AHW collection

On the Two Foot Gauge

Maine being one of the smaller states in the U.S. makes it seem like the logical place for North America's littlest railroads. With their tracks less than half as wide as most of the continent's lines, some of the Maine Two-Footers nevertheless kept going into the 1940s hauling fuel, feed and other supplies in little wooden cars that had to be loaded and unloaded by hand from regular freight cars, usually parked across platforms.

In Franklin County, Maine ran the Bridgton & Harrison, connecting with a branch of the standard gauge Maine Central at Bridgeton Jct. Farmers and small industries along the way depended on the B&H to haul their supplies in and finished goods out. Towards the end, people came from miles around to see and ride this anachronism. All the attention helped ensure that much of the antique equipment was eventually sold and preserved, including the engine on these pages which now resides on the Edaville Railroad.

(Above) Bridgeton & Harrison's Baldwin-built 2-4-4T No. 8 may seem like a small engine, but at 38 tons she's still quite a machine for three men to push around by hand. She was only 13 years old at the time of this 1937 picture. Since then her career on the tourist-hauling Edaville Railroad has spanned much longer. Three years after this photo she seemed to be doomed, as shop crews started stripping her of parts to keep older sister No. 7 going for the line's final year in 1941. Note the engineer's round rear-view mirror and the two lunch buckets on the running board.

(Right) Narrow gauge lines like the B&H were ideal for attracting fans because trains were slow, and crews friendly allowing for intimate contacts with the whole operation, as this portrait shows. Over two dozen hard core rail buffs have clambered aboard the tiny 2-4-4T No 8 on a summer day in 1938 to be recorded on this photo run-by for posterity. In the railroad's final years, a relatively small fee allowed visiting groups to practically run the show, stopping and going as wished.

(Right) Hey, old timer, bet you never thought the little narrow gauge would last long enough to bring these modern young folks out for a frolic and ride. His pipe gently tucked in hand, he _had_ to be part of this scene in more ways than one.
Four photos, Railway Negative Exchange/ AHW Collection

(Below) Here's No. 8 performing everyday chores, hauling fuel in little tanks and dry goods in the boxcars. You won't see the local folks out climbing the engine. They didn't know their little train would soon be bought by one of those fans - a chap with foresight named Ellis D. Atwood.

(Below) Ellis Atwood assembled equipment from five two-foot gauge lines in 1945, then surrounded his cranberry bogs at South Carver, Massachusetts with 5 1/2 miles of track on which his famous Edaville Railroad has operated successfully ever since. Among the five engines that run on the line is little B&H No. 8 (from our other photos), seen here on a winter doubleheader with its older sister, No. 7.
Edaville Railroad collections

Canadian Narrow Gauge
Steam and Diesel in Newfoundland

(Left) Here's a problem that sure fits the image some people have of Canada (not to mention what other Canadians have of Newfoundland!): "A dispatcher's nightmare!" says the photographer. "Confusion at Harry's Brook, on June 19, 1956." Newfoundland trackage was often inadequate to handle the traffic loads which occurred. A typical result is this scene at Harry's Brook - two freights meeting, plus two passenger trains, opposing sections of the 'Caribou,' all at the same time.

"Engine 902 was on a westbound freight. Engines 907 and 312 (shown) were on the eastbound. The eastbound 'Caribou' (right), behind engines 323 and 314 (both steam), was allowed by first. The westbound 'Caribou' is in the siding behind engine 305 and another 2-8-2. A great amount of see-sawing took place before this was settled, chewing up about an hour of schedule." This was at the time of transition from steam to diesel on the Newfoundland Railway (since 1949 under control of the government-owned Canadian National). Thus the unique narrow gauge steam-diesel doubleheader. Incidentally, this relatively-unknown 42-inch gauge line became North America's last regularly operating narrow gauge railroad during its final years in the 1980s, when it still ran freights over several divisions and mixed trains on its branchlines. The author has covered this line in one of his earlier books, so this photo is his only tribute to it in this volume.
R.J. Sandusky photo

(Below) Those few students of narrow gauge railroads who spent any time in Newfoundland seldom managed to reach the more remote connecting lines. Here, for instance, we're at Buchans Jct., Newfoundland in 1956, when there was still steam on the Island. In front of the station stands a northbound train of the Buchans Railway, with an ancient low-roofed baggage car at this end as a caboose, complete with open platforms. The light-coloured coach ahead of it just recently came here from the Toronto, Hamilton and Buffalo, where it was a gas-electric trailer. Southbound on the right is an equally interesting train, running on the Anglo-Newfoundland Co's Millertown Railway. The handsome little Plymouth engine was then No. 23, then later No. 100 of the Grand Falls Central and today is still in existence. The classic combine behind it was home made long ago and at this time furnished with streetcar seats. This train ran each day to Millertown Jct. to meet mainline narrow gauge passenger trains.
Alan Thomas photo/
R.J. Sandusky collection

(Above) Conductor Coates hands up train orders to the crew of Botwood Railway's Mikado No. 14. This was another narrow gauge shortline owned by the Anglo-Newfoundland Development Co. The well-kept line hauled freight and passengers into the 1950s with a handsome pair of modern 2-8-2s that barely showed their North British ancestry. The engines were painted greyish-black with orange trim and green drivers, mechanism and cab interior. They came here new as part of a larger order from the connecting mainline Canadian National. The train is about to leave Grand Falls for Botwood. The railway's station is on the right, the A.N.D. paper mill on the left. Note that these engines carried flangers mounted on their pilots.

(Below) Mixed trains meet on the Botwood Railway in Newfoundland. We're now aboard the train seen above, which has grown quite a bit since it left Grand Falls, with 16 loads of ore concentrate (iron, zinc, copper) and eight loads of newsprint in outside-braced boxcars, in addition to the combine (which is behind us.). The location is Peter's Arm Brook, halfway between Bishop's Falls and Botwood. The opposing train has just come from Botwood with sister No. 15 and another combine. Although these two photos were taken late in active narrow gauge history, the Buchans Mining ore cars seen here from the combine actually traversed *four* narrow gauge railways to reach their destination! They started on the Buchans Mining Co. line, then ran over the Millertown Railway, from there to the CNR's former Newfoundland mainline, and finally here on the Botwood Railway.

Both, R.J. Sandusky photos

An Industrial Narrow Gauge

The Kirkfield Crushed Stone Company

Here's proof that narrow gauge railroading doesn't need miles of mountain trackage nor fleets of mixed trains to be interesting. For some 50 years, the Kirkfield company operated a couple miles of 3 foot gauge track from their Lake Simcoe, Ontario quarry to a nearby rock crushing plant, using several 0-4-0 tankers and strings of 4-wheeled cars.

(Above right) The source of this little line's traffic was this rock quarry, along whose north wall we see Vulcan-built No. 4103 having its cars loaded by an electric power shovel. The shovel operator tooted an air whistle each time he wanted a car moved ahead. The scene was taken in September 1951.

(Above left) On a cold and bitter November day in 1957, one of the Vulcans works hard to lift 10 cars of rock out of the quarry pit. The average train was only eight cars long, so this one took some special effort.

(Below left) Narrow gauge meet of the tankers, recorded in 1951 with No. 4101 on the left blasting upgrade with a load, while 4103 passes with the empties headed down into the quarry.

(Below right) Cecil Holder has just filled the saddle tank of No., 4103 at the water tank, then pulled over to No. 2 track for his train of empties. While waiting for the last car, he takes time to oil the crosshead guides and check his running gear. Note the simple hook and chain coupling.

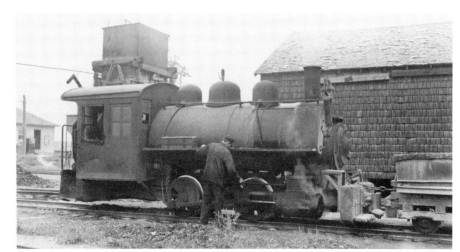

(Above right) Here are three of the several tankers used by Kirkfield over the years. On the left is Vulcan-built No. 1419, which began life in 1909 as Essex Constructing No. 1 (of Illinois). It is now at the Museum Village in Pickering, Ontario. Newer Vulcans 4103 and 4104, centre and right, later moved to the U.S. Photo was taken just after the usual Saturday noon shutdown in the summer of 1958.

(Below right) Overview of the narrow gauge facilities at the Kirkfield plant in September 1959, looking down from the stone crusher. Loaded cars were cabled up on the right, then descended to the left through a spring switch. Rerailing frogs stacked against the shed at the bottom indicate that the cars did not always cooperate. On the left is the shop track, while part of the quarry lies beyond. At far left is the Trent Canal, which is all that is left today of this scene. The line closed in 1960.

Both pages, Robert J. Sandusky photos

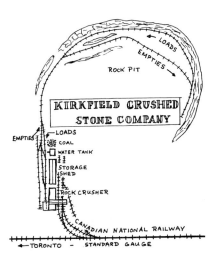

On the Canadian Prairies
The Alberta Railway and Coal Company

Narrow gauge railroading never caught on in the Canadian Rockies like it did in Colorado. Population was much smaller, mining more limited, and the transcontinental Canadian Pacific preferred to lay standard gauge tracks right from the start. But a few of its lines were built originally in three-foot gauge by earlier owners, including a sizeable network in southern Alberta, not far from the Rockies. The first segment of this was built in 1885 to haul coal from Lethbridge 108 miles to the CPR mainline at Medicine Hat. This later became a standard gauge part of the CPR's secondary mainline through the Crowsnest Pass and Kettle Valley. In 1890 a connection was built south from Lethbridge to the Great Falls and Canada Railroad, another narrow gauge line coming up from Montana. In 1900, a 47-mile narrow gauge branch was built to the town of Cardston, at the edge of the Blood Indian Reserve, near Waterton Lakes National Park, which is in the Canadian Rockies. Unfortunately, unlike the Colorado roads, these operations were hardly photographed. Besides, by 1909 the last of them had been converted to standard gauge, so their narrow gauge trains have been long gone.

(Above left) Here's one of 13 similar Baldwin-built narrow gauge Moguls that worked out of Lethbridge, Alberta back when the line east was called the Northwest Railway and Coal Company.

(Centre) This Alberta operation was not too great on keeping its equipment well-lettered or numbered, though otherwise it appears to have been in good condition. This Baldwin 2-8-0 does show the initials AR&C Co. on its tender, photographed around 1895 when the line was called the Alberta Railway and Coal Co., though locals knew it best as the "Turkey Trail" because of its narrow wandering tracks. The scene is thought to show the Great Falls, Montana narrow gauge enginehouse.

(Bottom) Here's downtown Lethbridge, Alberta in 1887 when it was only served by a narrow gauge railroad. A string of freight cars and two side-door cabooses are seen here at Lethbridge's first railroad station. Note the Mountie in striped trousers among the crowd. A modern Canadian city now stands at this place. Some of the equipment from this line was used in 1906 for the building of the famous Spiral Tunnels on the CPR's mainline through the Rockies. One of the Moguls fell into Sink Lake there and was left undisturbed for years. Its remains are now part of a nearby historical display.
Three photos, John Poulsen collection

British Columbia's Kaslo & Slocan Railway

Across the Rockies and further west in Canada from the Alberta narrow gauge lines ran the 29-mile Kaslo & Slocan, which was destined to join them in becoming part of the standard gauge Canadian Pacific Railway. This three-foot gauge track was built in the early 1890s as part of the Great Northern Railway's attempt to rush into southern British Columbia during a mineral boom. For some 20 years the small trains hauled supplies, people and silver-lead ore from the mountain town of Sandon, along with a few other places, to the docks at Kaslo on Kootenay Lake, where steamboats made connections with the GN's standard gauge line from Bonners Ferry, Idaho. Switchbacks, steep grades and many trestles were a constant challenge, along with deep snow, landslides, floods and finally a forest fire. In 1911 the K&S was sold to some Kaslo people for $25,000, they in turn selling it the the CPR whose crews rebuilt most of it to standard gauge the next year. The line had an interesting assortment of cars, along with a pair of Moguls bought second-hand from Alberta and a heavier Consolidation.

(Above) A Kaslo & Slocan Railway mixed train has stopped at Whitewater, B.C. and everyone from front to back is out to oblige the visiting photographer in this 1898 scene. One of the Moguls is trailed by coach No. 3, combine No. 4, and three home-made ore boxcars.
B.C. Archives photo No. B-7158

(Left) Train time on the Kaslo & Slocan at the station in Sandon, B.C. in 1904, four years after the original town had burned down. Although the place was rebuilt, the railroad suffered other problems until the section to here was closed down in 1909.
B. C. Archives photo No. D-5267

(Opposite, top right) Other end of the line on the K&S was here at the wharf in Kaslo, B.C., on the mountainous shores of Kootenay Lake. A sawmill and its boom of logs is in the foreground, while the narrow gauge railroad station is just beyond the two steamboats tied up on the right. A box-car stands to the right of it and three more freight cars are in between the two sets of boats.
John Poulsen collection

(Bottom right) Looking at the same area, we see Mogul No. 2 and a combine pulled up alongside a big sternwheeler.
John Poulsen collection

(Top left) The same area again, but this time looking down from the town itself at the Kaslo station and tracks, with a mixed train on the left and an ore boxcar near the water.
Harold K. Vollrath collection

Kaslo on Kootenay Lake

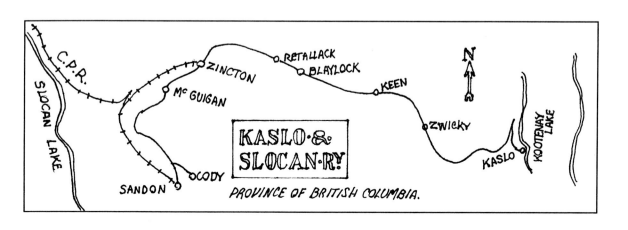

KASLO·&·SLOCAN·RY

PROVINCE OF BRITISH COLUMBIA.

Way Up North....
From B.C. to Alaska

(Opposite) This is about the closest Canada came to having narrow gauge railroading in the style of the Colorado Rockies. We're on the Kaslo & Slocan Railway in southeastern B.C.'s Selkirk range. Some of the crew and passengers have posed on the front of their train, as it sits on the dramatic curve at Payne Bluff, a few miles from Sandon. Several landslides in places like this caused the line to be abandoned within a few years.

B.C. Archives photo No. 5235

(Right) What might seem to be another spot along the same railroad is actually in the Skagway River valley of Alaska, on North America's northernmost narrow gauge line, the White Pass & Yukon Route, built in the 1890s to connect parts of the Yukon and British Columbia with the port in Skagway, Alaska. Although freight service ended on this rugged railway in the 1980s, passenger trains still carry tourists aboard a fleet of antique coaches, sometimes hauled by 2-8-2 No. 73, the line's last operable steam engine.

Canadian Pacific Corporate Archives collection

An Island Logger

B.C. Forest Museum's
Cowichan Valley Railway

(Opposite) Deep in the lush green forests of Canada's Vancouver Island runs the mile and a half long Cowichan Valley Railway, which is home to a couple of three-foot gauge tankers, an heirloom Shay, plus an assortment of odd little cars and gasoline powered engines. It is the perfect prototype for a model railroader with which to fill a spare room or garage corner. This scene shows the CVR in 1982, with two of the steamers fired up in front of the shop, while another peers into the open-air enginehouse where gas powered No. 26 rests on one of the tracks.

(Left) Hillcrest Shay No. 1 (built 1920) and 18 ton saddle tanker No. 25 (built by Vulcan in 1910) doze in the early morning mist, steamed up and ready for tourist hauling work later in the day. A retired logger named Gerry Wellburn first began to assemble this equipment back in the mid-1950s as a hobby, with historical foresight, when it might otherwise have gone off to scrap. Like a model railroader in full scale, he built a backyard line called the Glenora & Western. In 1965 he teamed up with forest industry departments and the B.C. government, to move his railroad along Highway 1 at Duncan, B.C., where they set up an operation widely known for its own charm and character.

(Below) No. 1 son (AHW IV) tries out CVR four-wheeled caboose No. 10 for size, back in 1978, just after his dad had brought home a much bigger one from the CPR. Although mostly "scratch built" by Wellburn, this car nonetheless illustrates a style typical of many small operations.
Both pages, AHW photos

(Above) Plymouth built this 8-ton gas mechanical engine in 1926 for industrial service. Now painted green and numbered 26, it is the queen of the Cowichan Valley Railway's small fleet of non-steam locomotives, serving as shop switcher on this fall day in 1984. Two-track open air engine house is at the back.

(Opposite) Three views of 12-ton 0-4-0 tanker No. 24, built by Vulcan in 1906. It began life as Pittsburgh Eastern No. 12, then moved to B.C. and became Crownest Coal No. 9, later Elk River Colliery No. 4. Brought to Vancouver Island as a worn out coal burner, she was converted to use oil with the addition of a small tender and fuel tank, then overhauled with many replacement parts.
Both pages, AHW photos

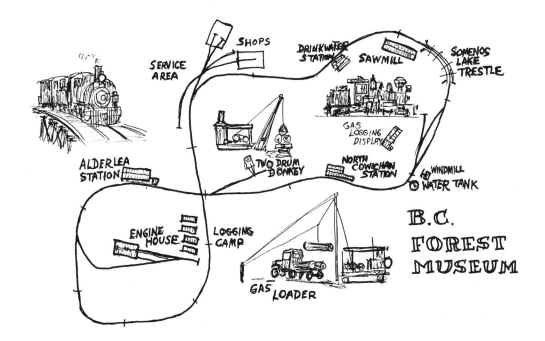

Tribute to a Special Little Shay

(Far lower right) As a teenager in search of surviving steam, this was my first view of Hillcrest No. 1 on a rainy afternnon in 1963. A freind had told me where to find her, employed by the Osborne Bay and Wharf Company, where she switched freight cars on a wooden dock during the odd times when a ship came in. Alas, at the time of my brief visit there was no ship in sight, nor any train crew. The little 25-ton Shay sat all alone by a locked white shed, her tender filled with coal and her fresh paint shining. Hanging from one of the valves inside the cab was a little tin sign that warned: "Remove cover from stack before lighting fire."

(Near right) For years afterwards I was sorry to have missed this little jewel in action. Nearly 20 years passed before we met again and this time her trim boiler was filled with steam. Originally built as a narrow gauge woodburner for the Hillcrest Lumber Company, but standard gauged for many years, her wheels were back to three foot width as the star attraction at B.C.'s Forest Museum. Engineer Spike Carson took me through the woods in her cab and let me blow the melodious whistle.

(Far upper right) My son Okan picked up his dad's fondness for Shays and small engines, finding Hillcrest No. 1 quite to his liking right from the start. Soon after that, Spike Carson offered the boy firing lessons, so the two spent a memorable weekend together. "When I was a boy about your age," Spike told him, "this engine was still a woodburner, like a lot of others here on the Island. I've had many splinters in my hands helping out with the work, riding in engine cabs just like you." Spike spent the best part of his life as engineer on the steam powered Alberni Pacific Lumber railway. "Running around on this bit of museum track is plain fun now, in my retirement age," he said. Okan has an H0n3 model of the engine to help keep alive the memory.

(This page, left) Winding her way through the curves of the Forest Museum trackage, Hillcrest No. 1 should feel right at home, having spent most of her life on various logging lines. After 14 years with Hillcrest, she went to the Export Lumber Co., then in 1947 she became Mayo Bros. Timber No.1, moving from there to the Osborne Wharf job.

(Below) Among scenic highlights along the Forest Museum line is this curved wooden trestle which brings passengers out over the edge of Somenos Lake, where wild birds are often seen. This kind of railroading is not much work for a geared engine, even with the small size of No. 1.
Both pages, AHW photos.

Sumpter Valley Railway
Oregon's "Stump Dodger"

In eastern Oregon the three-foot gauge Sumpter Valley Railway began laying tracks from the town of Baker to logging areas in the Blue Mountains, reaching Sumpter in 1896. By 1910 there were 80 miles of mainline, which included three summit crossings above 5,000 ft. in elevation. Because early track laying followed the cutting of timber, the line became locally known as the "Stump Dodger." Among its traffic were logs, cattle, passengers, and gold ore from a booming mining industry. Several private logging railroads connected with the SV and provided a lot of its traffic. Still, things slowed down after the Depression, with passenger service cancelled in 1937 and the railroad folding up altogether 10 years later.

In 1976 a bit of the old "Stump Dodger" was reborn, as a new Sumpter Valley Railroad began running tourist trains over some of the original right of way, using former W.H. Eccles Lumber Co. No. 3, a narrow gauge Heisler similar to those that once actually worked the line. In 1977 two of the original engines - Mikados 19 and 20 - were brought back to Oregon from the White Pass & Yukon R.R. in Alaska. Also returned to the SV from private owners was former coach No. 20, which is now restored and in operation.

(Left) Among the Sumpter Valley Railway's distinctions was its fleet of cabbage-stacked wood burning locomotives, including this fairly modern Mikado. No. 20 is seen here at Baker, Oregon in May 1937. It and sister No. 19 are back on SV property, undergoing repairs for tourist operations.

(Below) The SV mainline is seen in 1947 going past the mill town of Austin, Ore., with water tank on the right and an enginehouse at left.

(Right) Here's another narrow gauge survivor, one of the many illustrated in this book. Handsome wooden caboose No. 5 was built in October 1926 and is seen here at Baker in June 1947. Later, it spent many years sitting without wheels at the Eastern Oregon Museum in Haines, a few miles from Baker. Now back on home tracks, No. 5 was given new wheels during a rebuilding for tourist service.

(Below) This Sumpter Valley yard scene was taken during the final months of operations in 1947. It shows a big stacked wood burning Heisler stopped at the water tank with an empty flat car, while adjacent flats hold loads of fresh lumber, indicating that one of several sawmills is nearby. Note the slabs of firewood at the right. The Heisler that now operates on the revived Sumpter Valley once worked like the one in this photo, for the W.H. Eccles Lumber Co. along the old main line.
Both pages, Railway Negative Exchange/AHW Collection

(Left) Baldwin Ten-wheeler No. 50 was the Sumpter Valley's main passenger engine, bought around 1915 and seen here at Baker in May 1937. This engine, plus three of five Mikados that had also been bought back then, were sold to the Peruvian Government when the line closed in 1947.

(Below) Coach-combine No. 26 is seen at Baker with broken windows, facing an uncertain future after the line's closure. Since then it has found a new life on Alaska's famous White Pass & Yukon RR, where it resides with a whole fleet of historic narrow gauge coaches.

(Below left) Near the end of a 10 year stint in Oregon, famous Unitah narrow gauge Mallet No. 250 is seen at the Sumpter Valley shops in Baker, Oregon not long before she and sister 251 were dismantled, shipped to Portland, then loaded aboard the S.S. "Coastal Adventurer" for their trip south to Guatemala. See the picture of this engine at Escuintla on another page.

Both pages, Railway Negative Exchange/AHW Collection

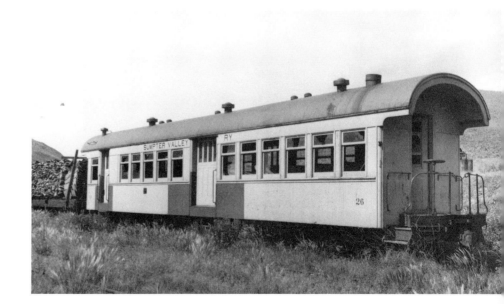

(Above) "Fireproofed," says a note on the back of this print from circa 1915, showing a narrow gauge two-truck Shay on what is thought to be the Clio Lumber Co.'s line in eastern Plumas County, California. Engine was a woodburner, thus the unique "spark-arrestor" attached to the stack, with side-delivery cinder disposal. The fireman's side is sometimes called the "off-side" of a Shay because photographers generally preferred showing the upright cylinders and connections to the geared wheels peculiar to this type of engine, but carried only on the engineer's side.
Western Pine Ass'n/AHW Collection

Nevada Country Narrow Gauge Railroad

California's Mother Lode country has been home to a number of interesting narrow gauge lines over the years, none more so than the NCNG at Grass Valley. Started in 1875 with a couple of brand new Baldwin three-foot gauge engines (4-4-0 "Grass Valley" and 2-6-0 "Nevada"), four passenger cars, plus 15 box and seven flat cars, the 22 mile pike was built for half a million dollars to serve as a transportation lifeline for people living and working around the old gold mining towns of Colfax, Grass Valley and Nevada City. Its operation was a family and community affair; schedules were leisurely; everyone seemed to be friendly.

But by the time these photos were taken, the people in the area had mostly gotten used to depending on cars and trucks, figuring it was cheaper to maintain roads and highways than the light and winding narrow gauge tracks. In fact, beginning in 1935, already the company itself offered customers truck and bus service, thus helping to put its own trains out of work. Passenger service ended in 1938 (with a Railway Historical Society fan trip); the rest of the line shut down in 1942. Wartime scrap prices made the railroad seem to be worth more dead than alive.

Today's folks along the old Nevada Country Narrow Gauge Railroad are trying to rectify that, having slowly reclaimed a few surviving bits of the railroad.

(Left) It's 1937 and you're looking over the cab roof of Nevada County Narrow Gauge No. 9 entering a curve through this rock cut.

(Opposite above) Chicago Park is certainly a fancy name for this barely populated water stop along the 22 mile California narrow gauge. 1882 Baldwin built 2-8-0 No. 8 is stopped for a drink in March 1941.

(Opposite below) A year later we again see No. 8 with a short freight train, parked by the engine house at Grass Valley; this was one of the very last trains to operate. The engine was originally D&RGW No. 283. A few weeks after this picture was taken, No. 8 was sold to the Plaster City Railroad down along the Mexican border, where she worked until being scrapped in 1950.
Both pages, Railway Negative Exchange/AHW collection

(Below) Locomotives were turned at one end of the line on this unique turntable near Colfax, California. No. 8 is seen from the top of a boxcar in 1938.

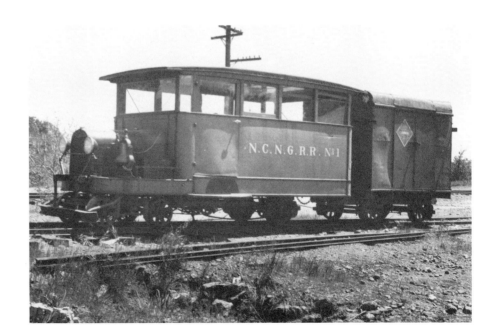

(Opposite, top) This beautiful 1875 Baldwin Mogul is one of the nicest old narrow gauge engines still around - now back in its home town of Nevada City. While some of today's Colorado engines were still pretty new back when this 1939 photo was taken, No. 5 was already considered an antique. Originally built as No. 1 of the Carson & Tahoe Railroad, this engine was saved from worse fate by its 1942 sale to the Frank Lloyd Studio of Hollywood. Unfortunately, they used her mainly to dramatize an "authentic train wreck" in the John Wayne movie "The Spoilers," after which she was pretty spoiled alright, having been forceably rolled on her side. Still, the 26 ton engine's remains were left to rust on a backlot, from where she was trucked back to Mother Lode in 1985 and is being cosmetically restored for an imaginative local railroad museum exhibit.

(Lower left) While the railfan crowd keeps its focus on the excursion train beyond, with No. 8, a few fellows like Bill Pennington are prowling around looking for relics such as this old Ford railcar to expose their films on. Homemade snowplow stands behind.

(Lower right) Railbus No. 10 was used in the closing years to provide light service when a whole train wasn't needed.

(Right) Travellers through California's Mother Lode country today can try to figure out where this scene was taken, showing 2-8-0 No. 8 with a short freight in April 1941. It's near Nevada City. Imagine the great Shell Oil Co. shipping its fuel in little truss-rod narrow gauge tank cars like those two behind the engine.

(Below) The turntable at Grass Valley was the standard form, with gallows suspension and "armstrong" turning.

All photos, Railway Negative Exchange/AHW collection.

Will Whittaker on the Nevada County Narrow Gauge in 1937

(Left) It's hard not to think what a fabulous community railroad operation this would be once again today, had the Nevada County Narrow Gauge Railroad somehow ridden out a couple more decades. Imagine these two engines and some of the old rolling stock placed inside this roomy sheet metal engine house at Grass valley and kept safely there until today.
The shot was taken on the morning of May 23, 1937, right after the photographer arrived in Grass Valley to experience his very first fan trip - a notable occasion for a man who has since travelled and photographed on trains all over the continent, as evidenced by his many credit lines.

(Top right) The fan trip on that May day in 1937 was for members of the Railway and Locomotive Historical Society who had chartered the line's newest and most powerful locomotive - 1914 Baldwin 2-8-0 No. 9 - for a day's outing over the 22 miles of trackage. Imagine fans of today climbing all over their favorite engine like this, prior to departure!

(Lower left) Perhaps the most spectacular piece of the NCNG was this crossing of the Bear River, where the special train has stopped to allow for a unique photograph. The structure stood until 1963, when crews with dynamite and machinery spent a week tearing it down.

(Lower right) Back in the days when railroads treated fans as friends, who in turn accepted their own responsibilities and didn't threaten legal action at the first sign of mishap. Nevertheless, one has to wonder what the fellow sitting on an overturned pail at the front of the lead coach's roof intended to do if the train's wheels should suddenly stick. How about the fellow in a suit hanging from the cab window; maybe to hold up the guy on the cab roof? Imagine today's insurance agents coming up with a premium for this?
All photos, W.C. Whittaker

Diamond & Caldor Railway

(Left) It took 63 trestles for these engines to make the 34 mile trip from Diamond Springs, California to Caldor. The D&C began hauling passengers and freight over its complete route in 1904, connected to the outside world through Southern Pacific tracks not far from the site of these pictures. Grades were steep and curves tight, with much of the traffic from logging, so the road naturally took a liking to geared power. Three of the line's Shays are visible here at the Diamond Springs engine house. No. 6 at left was a three truck wood burner when new in 1909, although the D&C changed to fuel oil the next year. No. 4, on the right, is a lighter two truck Shay built in 1907, displayed today in nearby Placerville. Railbus No. 10 was bought by Hal Wilmunder and operated for some years on his private Camino, Cable and Northern in Roseville. Shay No. 10 is barely visible behind the railbus.

(Above) A midday scene at Diamond Springs during July 1951 finds two other Shays parked with No. 10. At left, No 7 was built in 1912, No. 8 in 1917, the latter engine being used to dismantle the D&C in the summer of 1953, after which all three of these engines were scrapped.

(Facing page) A farewell scene in the spring of 1953, about the time the Diamond & Caldor Railway shut down. Beyond the water tank, to the right, is part of the light-painted cab and chassis of a new standard gauge diesel switcher being sort of "scratch built" (on a Sacramento Northern electric engine chassis) to serve the local Caldor Lumber Company after shut down of the narrow gauge. How many logging operations today would leave a fine big tree like the one at left standing in such a convenient spot?

Three photos, RNE/AHW Collection

Michigan California Lumber Co.

(Above left) Two truck Shay No. 9 was still a woodburner at the time of this 1942 scene taken by the square water tank in one of Mich-Cal's logging camps. The line had less than 10 years left to operate.
Francis Guido photo/W.C. Whittaker collection

(Below left) Michigan-California Lumber Company No. 2 was the oldest operating Shay at the time of this May 1949 photo at Camino, California. The 13 ton machine was built by Lima as a woodburner in 1884 for the Rumsey Lumber Co. of Michigan. A few years later she worked for another Michigan logging line before moving in 1901 to work on the El Dorado Lumber Co., which later became Mich-Cal Lbr. in 1918. For a while No. 2 was a mainline engine working between South Cable and Camino on grades up to 7%, often with a small Climax as helper. Replaced in 1904 by heavier Shay No. 7, she then became the Camino mill switcher, a job she held two more years after this photo. Today she is the oldest Shay in existence, on display not far from where she worked so long.
W.C. Whittaker photo

(Above) Once a common scene in California forests, fresh logs are being hauled to the mill aboard short, sturdy cars in charge of Michigan-California Shay No. 6. A daring brakeman is getting a memorable ride on the single large log, the third car back.
Ernie Plant Collection

(Above) Steam and smoke add drama to this 1942 scene at Michigan-California's Pino Grande mill, where wood burning Shay No. 5 has just dumped a trainload of logs into the millpond below.
Railway Negative Exchange/AHW Collection
(Opposite, top) A note with this photo says we're looking from the tender of Michigan-California Shay No. 10, running backwards with 25 carloads of logs, taken near Camp 10 in 1942. That sounds like quite a train, although Mich-Cal's cars were short and the loads were fairly light. Note that the logs are not tied down at all, which must have led to some interesting results over rough sections of track.
Railway Negative Exchange/AHW Collection
(Opposite, below) Wonder what sort of insurance premiums would be needed to run an excursion like this one, today? Michigan-California's antique Shay No. 2 leads this double-headed fantrip across one of the line's several curved trestles in 1938. If you look carefully, there's still one or two vacant spots where more riders could have perched, even next to the fellows up on the cab roof.
W.C. Whittaker photo

West Side Lumber Company

Nine Shays and five Heislers have graced the rosters of this line, which became famous as the last narrow gauge logging railroad operating in 1960, shut down the following year. The locomotives and much of the rolling stock in use at the end have been saved and preserved, although several efforts to turn parts of the original line into a tourist railroad came to nothing, with all track gone and the equipment widely dispersed. The engine featured on these two pages, built new for West Side in 1923, still sees occasional operation on the Midwest Central Railroad in Mt. Pleasant, Iowa.

(Left) Night Train for Tuolume. Looking somewhat like an HO model on a well-scenicked layout, West Side Lumber Company Shay No. 9 is frozen in time with her load of logs as the photographer's battery of flashes goes off at trackside some ways out of town. The blinding lights must have left a strong impression on the crew as they got near home after another long and tiring run into the hills for more trees to feed the company's mill. Most West Side men enjoyed the special attention, pleased to help photographers wanting to record what they knew would soon come to an end.
Richard Steinheimer photo

(Right) Here's West Side No. 9 again, in August 1957, captured in a romantically beautiful scene the photographer has titled "A Monument to Fred." He says: "The Clavey River bridge, engineered and built by Fed Ellis, president of the West Side for many years. Shay No. 9 with engineer Bert Bergstrom eases her loads over the curved structure in the hot mid day sun. She'll rest here for a long drink of spring water, then on to Deadwood."
John S. Anderson photo

West Side Lumber Company

(Left above) Logging railroads often accumulated varied and interesting collections of second-hand and home-made equipment; in that regard the West Side Lumber Co. was quite typical. What made this line more remarkable is that it survived long enough for the historic value of its engines and rolling stock to be appreciated. As a result, most of it has survived, some of it still operating here and there. This 1941 view shows a homemade snowplow whose trucks have heavy wooden beams for bolsters. The hump-backed flatcar behind it has link-and-pin couplers, some of which stayed in use till the end. The unnumbered caboose is one of several short, custom-built models used on the West Side over the years.

(Left below) The West Side's railroad began in 1898 as the common carrier Hetch Hetchy and Yosemite Valley, with grand dreams to serve those two widely-acclaimed scenic places. The wooden building on the right was that railroad's Tuolumne depot and office. The dual gauge trackage ran only a bit beyond this scene, but the mainline of the narrow gauge portion, leading from the sawmill behind us, went left and out into the woods. The three-stall wooden building beyond served as West Side's car shops.

Both photos, W.C. Whittaker

(Opposite) Here we are inside those same car shops, back in the final years of their operation during the 1950s. Among previous owners of West Side equipment were such California narrow gauge lines as the Butte & Plumas Ry., Sierra Nevada Wood & Lumber Co., and the Swayne Lumber Co. My first visit to the West Side was during high school summer vacation in 1961, which was unfortunately just a few months after the last narrow gauge trains had tied up in Tuolumne. All the equipment was still on hand - pending the outcome of a trial season hauling logs with trucks instead of trains. Walking past strings of old cars and quiet Shays, I entered this car shop building, which was deserted but otherwise looked almost exactly the same as in this scene. Tools and supplies were neatly on hand, waiting for workmen to return, though they never did. By one large workbench hung a pencilled note reading, "Check journals on car 145," parked nearby. Hope whoever bought it afterwards got the note with it.

John S. Anderson photo

(Left) The photographer has captured here the essence of 1950's West Side railroading with this classic and favorite shot showing Shay No. 12 and caboose No. 6 on the curved Niagara Creek bridge, approaching a water tank, with bunkhouses for the loggers in the woods behind Shay No. 12 is now on the Georgetown Loop RR in Colorado.

For me, this photo is in particular a tribute to the caboose itself, which is still in existence and privately owned. While assembling my book *Rails in the Mother Lode* during the early 1960s, I spent some time studying and photographing the recently-retired narrow gauge equipment. This caboose became my favorite, especially after I sat out a vivid thunderstorm inside of it one afternoon. When I brashly asked at the office about buying this car (I was still in high school), the answer was, "$150 bucks." For a couple of years I tried to figure out where to put it if I bought it, then somebody else did (and moved it to Chama for a while!), which answered the question. It took another 20 years before I fulfilled my own desire with a bigger one from the CPR.

John S. Anderson photo

Heisler No. 3
From the West Side Lumber Co. to the
Roaring Camp & Big Trees R.R.

(Right) Those of us who just missed seeing the West Side Lumber Company's last narrow gauge trains for a while had the consolation of watching Heisler No. 3 switching standard gauge trackage around the Tuolumne mill. Built in 1899 for narrow gauge (one of four Heislers on the West Side, along with nine Shays and three Tankers), this engine got standard gauge trucks in 1948, but is now back again to narrow gauge. It is seen here crossing Turnback trestle in the 1950s.
W.C. Whittaker photo

(Below) Here's the same Heisler today (on the right) at home on the Roaring Camp Narrow Gauge Railroad, where the spirit of narrow gauge logging and railroading appears to be alive and well. In the left stall sits an old friend and work-mate, former West Side three-truck Shay No. 7. In between is two-truck Shay No. 1, the "Dixiana," brought from a narrow gauge logging outfit in the south. The Roaring Camp line runs through historic Big Trees Ranch, in old time narrow gauge country. It opened to traffic in 1963 through the efforts of F. Norman Clark, rolling through groves of gigantic redwoods in the style of California logging railroads of the past. Six steam engines are now on the Roaring Camp roster, pulling a variety of interesting cars over the six mile trackage. Incidentally, not too far away is another scenic line that operates with narrow gauge equipment - the Yosemite Mountain and Sugar Pine RR - using former West Side Shays 10 and 15 on four miles of trackage just outside Yosemite National Park.
Roaring Camp & Big Trees photo

John Anderson
On the West Side

Although numerous scenes of action at the West Side mill in Tuolumne were recorded, few photographers braved the rough roads and uncertain schedules required to capture West Side's logging trains operating in the woods. Among the most ambitious and successful of these hardy ones was John Anderson, well known for his brass model work at Kemtron, who liked to spend weekends camping along the West Side line during the 1950s. He was introduced to this practice by pioneer West Side fan - and fellow Kemtron worker - Ken Hatheway, who preferred to shoot movies while John took black and white stills. In later years they were so accepted by the West Side men that they often slept in the logger's cabins and ate at their cookhouses.

(Left) During a water stop at Clavey tank with No. 14 on July 27, 1957, fireman John Wyhlidko polishes the brass bell while engineer Jim Weeks keeps him company.
(Below) A self portrait of the intrepid photographer on the back of Shay No. 7 at Camp 45 on Sept. 8, 1956.

(Above right) Another scene of No. 14 at the Clavey tank, a routine stopping place for water. In later years, the West Side operated in two divisions, the "town side" (between Tuolumne and Camp 24) and the "woods side" (between Camp 45 and Camp 24). Normally, the two divisions would stage meets at Camp 24 twice a day. These photos of the No. 14 show it returning to Camp 45 shortly after having met the town train at Camp 24. This was the first train of the day; it had left Camp 45 shortly after midnight to meet the town train at 6 a.m., exchanging its loads for a train of empties plus tank car No. 4, full of diesel fuel for the cats and trucks in camp.

(Below right) After taking water, No. 14 and its train crosses Clavey Bridge on the way back to Camp 45, where its arrival will allow the next train of logs to head for the second meet of the day at Camp 24. On the way back, the engine will take fuel at Crumbine, then turn on the wye there and back into camp in order to be ready for its next trip to Camp 24 the following night.
Both pages, John S. Anderson photos,
Timothy S. McCartney collection

Pacific Coast Railway

Southern California is not generally known for narrow gauge railroading, yet one interesting line survived there until the 1940s. The Pacific Coast Railway had its start as a 2 1/2 foot gauge horse-drawn operation serving a wharf at Port San Luis, near San Luis Obispo, in the early 1870s. In the 1880s a steam powered 3-foot gauge line was built to connect the farm-rich Santa Maria Valley with this wharf. Train traffic increased with the discovery of oil in the region during the early 1900s, hauled aboard a fleet of homemade tank cars. Two branches were built, operated with home made electric engines and a second hand interurban car. But eventually highways came and took their toll, so the line was slowly dismantled during the 1930s, with the last of it gone by 1942.

(Left above) Fans from the Bay Area and Los Angeles found the Pacific Coast Railway close and easy to visit, as on this October day in 1940, with quite a crowd aboard the gondolas drawn by 2-8-0 No. 105. The location is Hedley Tower, near San Luis Obispo, where narrow gauge tracks crossed those of mainline Southern Pacific. The engine was built by Baldwin in 1904 and scrapped during the wartime drive for metal, a few years after the line closed.
W.C. Whittaker photo

(Below) Pacific Coast Railway Tenwheeler No. 110 is seen switching cars at San Luis Obispo on July 28, 1941 during the final season of operation. This was a sister engine to the 4-6-0s operated by Southern Pacific in the Owens Valley, bought second-hand in the 1920s from the Nevada-California-Oregon Railway after that line was standard gauged.
Railway Negative Exchange/AHW Collection

Narrow Gauge Slaughter House
in San Francisco
1939

(Above) This is what happened to many historic pieces of equipment back in the days when few people had the foresight and resources to interfere. These are engines from the Eureka-Nevada Ry., with the single diamond stack belonging to a doomed Nevada Central engine.

Railway Negative Exchange/AHW collection

Ward Kimball's
GRIZZLY FLATS
The Ultimate in a Backyard Railroad

For over 50 years Ward Kimball was President of a tiny narrow gauge line that operated "when needed" on his "estate" in the heart of Southern California. Three fabulous little steam engines hauled a covey of wooden carriages - all of them notably historic - on a bit of "branchline" complete with ornate depot, enginehouse, water tank, windmill, and spindly tracks. The whole operation seemed so unlikely that some who heard about it dismissed it as a "Hollywood fantasy," to which there was actually some truth.

But the Grizzly Flats Railroad stayed in business for over half a century without changing, which is a long time for any railroad operation, no matter what its background or reason. For that alone it deserves a place in the annals of narrow gauge railroading. But in addition, the G.F.R.R. has managed to preserve a certain "spirit" of narrow gauge railroading that other surviving operations often lost in the struggle just to maintain their equipment.

Ward Kimball is an artist; his Hollywood connection is the lifelong work he did for Walt Disney as the animator of famous characters such as Jiminy Cricket, and the friends of Dumbo. Disney's gift of the Grizzly Flats station, following a 1930s movie, helped form the nucleus of Ward's backyard railroad. That backyard itself - back then surrounded by orange groves - was somewhat like a canvas for this artist. On it he produced a very large work - as if he were Rembrandt or Michelangelo - except that his subject was a train. Throughout the years, critics and public alike have given that work nothing but rave reviews.

"The whole idea of having a backyard railroad started in the spring of 1937," said Ward Kimball, recalling a time when few people thought of preserving historic trains, especially near their own homes. "The Southern Pacific-owned Carson & Colorado was burning up a lot of their old passenger car equipment and, if you happened to know about this, any one of their antique day coaches could be purchased for $50.00, trucks and all. We thought that having a full-sized passenger coach in our back yard would made a unique bar of a railroad museum."

On that note, the family built a stub of track with some 35 pound rails and got ready to welcome the little 40-foot coach.

"Very suddenly, however, our ideas began to change. We heard that the Nevada Central Railroad was abandoning their line forever and had three or four old vintage locomotives for sale." It was the kind of chance to affect history that seldom comes twice - for the sum of $400, Ward Kimball saved the life of an 1881 Baldwin Mogul originally called the "Sidney Dillon." As Nevada Central No. 2, she had just finished bringing the last flat cars full of rails from the torn-up line. Within Kimball's Grizzly Flats "work of art," this engine became a rare masterpiece just by itself.

It cost $450 to have No. 2 hauled aboard a standard gauge Southern Pacific gondola from Nevada to Los Angeles, where S.P. shop forces gave it a thorough inspection and tune up. From there the engine and tender were trucked to the orange grove site, where friends had already helped lay additional track. Although the Grizzly Flats was created mostly from Ward Kimball's own fantasies, he was aided and abetted not only by wife Betty and their three children, but also by an active group of fellow artists and workers, including Walt Disney and noted rail historian, Gerald Best. This crew built a 40' x 60' Victorian style enginehouse at the lower end of the three foot gauge railroad, wherein to store the equipment and work on it.

"As soon as the enginehouse roof was completed, we coasted the passenger car and the locomotive to their side-by-side resting places," he fondly recalls. How many model railroaders daydream about doing such a thing? Instead of little kits in boxes, Ward and his friends had the real thing to work with. "We made out a complete repair list to make the old locomotive like new." For the next few years this group met regularly in their spare time, faithfully restoring the little narrow gauge train. They stripped old No. 2 down without shame, though they all treated her as a "lady." In fact, Kimball afterwards named her "Emma Nevada" in honour of a famous opera star who was born in that state and once made a triumphant homecoming aboard a special train pulled by this same little Mogul.

"The paint job was most fun of all, with three coats being applied. The colour scheme we chose was sort of a composite of early-day locomotives. The wheels are bright vermillion striped in gold leaf. Pilot, headlight and domes are finished in deep red and trimmed in gold leaf. Cylinder and steam chest covers are deep green with vermillion trim and gold leaf flower designs added. The cab is olive green trimmed in venetian red, with gold leaf lettering. Undercarriage and motion is painted black and red. Headlight pictures are painted in authentic style. Cab fittings are trimmed in red, green and black, with brass gauges kept in high polish. By way of contrast to our locomotive, the coach is finished in a bright canary yellow, with apple green letter boards, maroon-trimmed windows and gold filigree."

(Above) Walt Disney gives his "traditional engineer's pose" aboard the freshly restored 1881 Mogul "Emma Nevada" while his "fireman" - and employee - Ward Kimball looks out from the gangway. Walt Disney had quite a backyard railroad of his own for many years, home-built and with live steam. Later he fulfilled even grander fantasies by restoring a variety of old narrow gauge engines for his Disneyland and other ventures, in which Ward was also involved.
Ward Kimball Collection

(Opposite) Could be any little Western shortline of the late 1880s - a simple wooden enginehouse, some tools and work benches, and a pretty little Mogul sitting on light tracks. But this is a scene from the memorable 1960s, a time of near hibernation for Ward Kimball's backyard railroad; a time capsule, well taken care of.
AHW photo

Operations on the railroad were infrequent right from the start, but usually involved a special gathering or event. Student groups sometimes came by the busload; railfans were welcome if they called ahead. Magazines and newspapers wrote about it, such as LIFE Magazine's 1944 story, "Life goes to a Railroad Party," or a piece in the Aug. 1947 POPULAR MECHANICS called "Railroad Fans on the Loose." Ward Kimball used the railroad for inspiration in drawing the adventures of Casey Jr., a cartoon train in the Disney stories of Dumbo. Said he about the steam-ups of those days: "Our usual run consisted of four or five hours of back and forth travel on our 650 feet of roadbed. This may sound monotonous, but to a group of amateur railroaders such as we, this short run can be imagined to feel like a 50 mile jaunt." Is that not the essence of miniature railroading all over the world, spoken by someone used to expounding on small things?

With the passing of years, urbanization moved in on the Grizzly Flats RR, so its infrequent operations became even more seldom, especially after stricter smoke laws forced coal-burning Mogul No. 2 into retirement. However, by this time the line was home to not one, but three narrow gauge steam engines, two of them being wood burners whose smoke was still allowed. Eventually, Ward Kimball decided it was time to shut his backyard train operation down altogether, so in October 1990 the Grizzly Flats RR was conveyed to the well-known Orange Empire Railway Museum, not far away in Perris, California, where it can continue to be operated and appreciated by generations to come.

ANNOUNCING An
EXCURSION!

Over The GREAT PLEASURE ROUTE
OF THE
GRIZZLY FLATS R.R.

"THE SCENIC WONDER OF THE WEST"

SOUTHERN CALIFORNIA LIVE STEAMERS
Annual Field Day!
SUNDAY, AUGUST 24, 1947 — *Bring Your Picnic Lunch!*
Safety First! ☞ YOU ARE RESPONSIBLE FOR YOUR OWN CHILDREN
WARD KIMBALL, PRES., 1616 ARDENDALE AVE., SAN GABRIEL, CALIF.

☞ **LIGHTENING EXPRESS TRAIN!** ☜

It is DECIDEDLY TRUE that in Aggregate of Mileage, Perfection of Construction, Magnificence of Equipment, Excellence of Accommodations, and Carefulness of Management the GRIZZLY FLATS R.R. Company's System of Lines is unrivalled, while the TIME made by its Trains, and SCENERY They Traverse, are ➳ Unsurpassed on the American Continent!

WARNING!
NO SHOOTING of BUFFALO, PRAIRIE DOGS, CHILDREN, or other WILD GAME from the CHAIR CAR Windows while Train is in Motion

HEALTH, PLEASURE, COMFORT.

(Above) Tiny Grizzly Flats station was modelled by Walt Disney crews to resemble an old Lehigh Valley RR depot for the film "So Dear to my Heart." Disney's gift of this building to his friend and employee helped inspire Ward Kimball to build his backyard railroad.
AHW photo

(Right) The Man with many Hats. Here's Ward Kimball inside the Grizzly Flats station, this time in the role of agent, perhaps pretending his little Mogul is due here soon with a mixed train from the gold mines. Parts of the building are furnished with authentic depot relics, the rest held some of Ward's antique toy trains, books and other memorabilia.
Ward Kimball collection

(Opposite page) Three eras in the life of Grizzly Flats No. 2, the "Emma Nevada." At lower left is the earliest photo known of the engine, standing ready at Battle Mountain, Nevada for its first run to Austin in 1881, when she was the Nevada Central Railroad's "Sidney Dillon."
Ward Kimball collection

(Lower right) More than 50 years later the engine is seen in the final days of the Nevada Central, looking rather worn, having lost her name and become simply No. 2.
Richard B. Jackson photo/Ward Kimball collection

(Opposite above) And there's that mixed train we were talking about at the depot. No. 2 is seen in her early moments of glory on the still-a-building Grizzly Flats RR in the early 1940s, when the area was surrounded by orange groves. Behind the engine is Carson and Colorado coach No. 5 and Pacific Coast Railway side-door caboose No. 4.
Ward Kimball photo

(Above left) Strange sounds were heard among the orange groves of San Gabriel, California in the early 1940s as bits and pieces of narrow gauge railroading moved into the sparsely settled neighborhood. At this time the Grizzly Flats still had modest plans, with only the Nevada Central Mogul and the Carson & Colorado coach on hand.

(Above right) Weekend railroaders turned the Kimball family backyard into a small railroad terminal over a period of several years, work sessions often ending in a playful barbecue. Here, the crew is raising up the new enginehouse, built as a composite of old-time plans. Crew members included I.A. Crawford, Bob and Tom Crawford, Bill Cooper, Art Rudd, Gerald Best, plus the owners. Notice the space for a locomotive repair pit on the right.

(Below right) Model railroaders on a grand scale - Ward Kimball (in bowler hat) guides his track crew, as they learn to handle the 35 pound rails salvaged from abandoned lines such as the Carson & Colorado. One piece of Central Pacific rail came to California from Holland and is marked 1850.

(Below left) Looking somewhat worse for wear is Waimanalo Sugar Co. No. 2, named the "Pokaa," which was shipped to the Grizzly Flats RR from Hawaii in 1948.

(Opposite) Here's the same little sugar plantation engine after a major rebuilding, completed in 1956. She now carries No. 1 for the GFRR, but is better known as "Chloe," also the name of the youngest Kimball daughter. Behind her is the "Olomana," an older sister of No. 1 brought from Hawaii at the same time by historian Gerald Best, who later donated this cute little Baldwin Tanker to the Smithsonian Institute where it is now on display in the Railroad Hall.

All photos from Ward Kimball

(Above) It's still cool this early in the morning in Southern California, as bright sunlight shines down on 0-4-2 Tanker No. 1, the "Chloe," being steamed up outside the Grizzly Flats enginehouse. While Mogul No. 2 and Tanker No. 3 rest in the shade inside, there's going to be a little action on the mainline here. White flags are up on the pilot of No. 1 indicating an Extra Train. Already a little candy-striped four-wheel car is hooked on behind, perhaps indicating the kind of revenue tonnage. Fuel for the engine is in the pile at right. Rare handcar on the ground once belonged to the Pacific Coast Railway.

GRIZZLY FLATS RAILROAD

WARD W. KIMBALL
President
BETTY L. KIMBALL
Vice Pres.

G. F. RR.

8910

Executive Offices
1476 ARDENDALL AVE.

THE SCENIC WONDER OF THE WEST

San Gabriel, Calif. Sept. 20 19 65

Dear Adolph:

Thanks very much for the fine photos of the "Brachs" scene. These will be added to my vast collection of Grizzly Flats Railroad memory photos, which some distant collector 50 years from now just won't believe.

I'll try to remember the Hetch-Hetchy photos.

Ward Kimball

WALT DISNEY PRODUCTIONS
500 SOUTH BUENA VISTA • BURBANK • CALIFORNIA

THANKS

FIREHOUSE FIVE PLUS TWO

* Grizzly Flats Footnote

One summer day in 1965 my dad came home from work and said that his boss had invited me to come to his house the next day to see a steam engine running. Not sure what to make of this, since I knew he lived in an exclusive Southern California suburb, I nevertheless brought my cameras early the next morning. It turned out the boss was living where orange groves used to grow, right across the street from the Grizzly Flats Railroad. What's more, this was to be one of the only revenue runs ever made by the line during its 50 some years in that location. The Brachs Candy Company "chartered" the train that day and brought out a film crew to shoot a "cute" little TV commercial, with girls doing the twist as the "Candyland Express" arrived. *Trains* Magazine and *Pacific News* both printed photos in their news sections from my cameras that day.

(Above) Technical preparations for filming these scenes took most of the day, but the train actually ran very little, so the "crew" had lots of chance to visit. That's "him" third from left, in the jungle fighter's outfit; Engineer, Fireman and Conductor Ward Kimball, shrugging about all the "operating delays." The older fellow in the suit is one of the railroad's "officials," Gerald M. Best, noted rail historian and author, owner of Tanker No. 3 parked inside the enginehouse. The film crew may have seen these men as a pair of eccentrics, not realizing what valuable pieces of history they were preserving. Flat bottom gondola No. 223 was bought from the Southern Pacific in 1960, when that railroad's narrow gauge line closed down in the desert. Beyond the water tank sits an 1890 boxcar bought from the Pacific Coast Railway when it closed down in 1946.

(Right) Lights, camera, action! The star of the day's show simmers quietly in the hot sun, while close-ups are being filmed of a "pretty girl" at the throttle (with Ward Kimball nearby, staying low and in the shadows). A few times the engine ran back and forth, ringing its bell and tooting the whistle. No doubt there were some interesting comments made in nearby pools and patios about the unusual neighbor and his peculiar passion.

Both pages, AHW photos

The Ghost Town & Calico R.R.
A Retirement Line in Southern California

To Ed Randow it must have been an incongruous sight - a pair of diamond stacked three-foot gauge Consolidations with a string of wooden coaches, equipment that first hauled miners and dance hall girls back in the Colorado of the 1880's and 90's - now rolling gently past palm trees and eucalyptus stands in the warm California sun. After all, Ed recalled more than a few times nearly freezing his hands and feet trying to keep those same engines running through the likes of Rocky Mountain blizzards, sometimes struggling to get their wheels back onto frozen tracks.

The Rio Grande Southern was only a memory by the time I got to know Ed. He'd worked on the line 40 years, serving as master mechanic when it finally shut down in 1951. Much of its antique equipment was scrapped soon afterwards, but engine 41 was brought west by Walter Knott, along with sister engine No. 340 (renumbered to 40) from the neighboring D&RGW, plus a fleet of cars that included three coaches (Nos. 310, 325 and 326), well-known parlor cars "Chama" and "Durango," RGS President Otto Mears' private car "Edna," caboose 0402, and some freight cars. Also in the GT&C fleet is Galloping Goose No. 5, one of several silver railbuses that rolled through the mountains on the RGS.

The idea of such a retirement life on the balmy Pacific Coast sounded good enough that Walter Knott even brought a couple of the RGS people back with him, including Ed Randow and his boss, the former RGS Road Superintendent R.R. Boucher, who traded operational headaches in the rugged Rockies for the easier pleasures of punching tickets presented by carefree tourists during 10 minute circle trips around Knott's Berry Farm.

Ed Randow was a slight, grey-haired man whose mechanical abilities relied more on skill than on brute strength. From Colorado he'd brought tools, blueprints and equipment notes, plus a wealth of anecdotes that he shared freely with those who cared to listen, including this teenaged boy. Once he'd been stuck for nearly a week in some snowed-in pass near Telluride, using coal from No. 41's tender to keep stoves going inside the two coaches so that the handful of passengers and crew wouldn't freeze to death before rescue. Tales like that <u>almost</u> made me understand why he said he didn't miss those days at all, though I often wished to experience them with him even just once, for a short little while.

There's no telling how many of us got our first taste of narrow gauge railroading at Knott's Berry Farm. My school years were spent not a half hour's drive from Buena Park, California, where Walter Knott had built his fabulous fantasy western village and railroad, using many genuine parts. In those days a ride on the train cost a quarter, but Ed gave me a Lifetime Pass so I often stayed aboard for several rounds. My favorite time for that was late at night, just before the Farm closed, when most tourists were gone and the darkness allowed for greater fantasizing. The wooden cars would squeak and groan as the engine up ahead puffed and steamed around tight curves over light rails - sounds and feelings that would have been the same while entering places like Rico and Durango 50 or 75 years earlier.

Upon graduating from high school I joined the Knott's payroll as a helper, Ed Randow offering to train me in my spare time as a fireman. But my career on steam was cut short by the more tempting offer of being a fireman on the diesels of real-life Union Pacific, where I worked my way through college.

Since those days, this little narrow gauge operation has seen some dramatic changes, including high fences and the replacement of lawns and palm trees by modern amusement rides. Interestingly, while the setting has become flashier, the engines and train lost some of the gaudiness applied by Ed and his crew in initial efforts to please the tourists. With time having increased the appreciation for the train's history, both engines were restored to their last real working appearances, with black paint and silver smokeboxes, rather than bright colors, old-style stacks and big headlights. Now that their old haunts of Durango and Chama are such successful historical operations, perhaps someday we'll see this circle completed and the antique trains back in their original environment. Imagine heading up Cumbres Pass behind Nos. 40 and 41 doubleheaded, or even just chugging slowly with one of them through the Chama yard.

(Opposite) Ed Randow is firing former D&RGW No. 340 on a test run after major shop work in 1960, when I was still a boy thinking it might be fun to work up there myself someday. Scenes like this have inspired countless tourists and travellers at Knott's Berry Farm with thoughts of old-time railroading over the 40-some years that this successful line has been in operation.
AHW photo

(Left) An early summer morning in 1962 finds Ghost Town and Calico No. 41 simmering softly outside the wooden engine house, waiting for weekday train service to start at 11. Galloping Goose No. 5 sits in clean silver paint as if it just got in from the Ophir Loop. Parts of Walter Knott's original Ghost Town are in the park-like area behind. The engine house is long gone, as are the tracks from this spot. This scene is now history, since Knott's Berry Farm built a large, modern amusement area across here.
AHW photo

(Below) No. 464 is one of two Class K-27 Mikados left, having last worked for the D&RGW as Durango yard switcher around 1960. After several years of sitting neglected near the roundhouse, this engine was shipped to Knott's Berry Farm to join the two Consolidations. Seen here being unloaded at the tourist line's modern shop, crews soon had this noted "Mudhen" running, but found it too large for the park's trackage. No. 464 then went to the Huckleberry Railroad in Michigan, where she still operates.
Knotts Berry Farm Photo

(Right) This special drama of narrow gauge railroading took place early one foggy morning in the Autumn of 1959 by request of the photographer, who was then 15. Ed Randow was a railroad man who went strictly by the books, which in California included a prohibition against making smoke with steam engines. Normally that was no problem for these two at Knott's Berry Farm, where - instead of climbing mountain passes and bucking blizzards - they just rolled around the level park in balmy weather all day.

Every couple of weeks Ed and his crew would switch engines, taking one out of service for tune ups and repairs. This required both engines to be fired up, in order to get around each other on the limited trackage. When I asked him to pose the two side by side with plumes of smoke, he gave me ten seconds, which the fireman later told me he watched carefully on his regulation Hamilton. Even the boys back in Durango couldn't have done much better than this.

Incidentally, this was the first photograph I ever had published, having sent a print of it to Freeman Hubbard at RAILROAD Magazine. He sent me a short note of congratulations on getting my first "byline" and encouraged me to send something more. He was an inspiration to many writers and documenters of the railroad scene. I dedicate this picture to his memory.

(Below) Here's No. 41 exactly 20 years earlier, balanced on the Rio Grande Southern turntable at Ridgeway. Knott's Berry Farm crews in recent years have restored the engine close to this appearance, which is an interesting evolution.
Mallory Hope Farrell Collection/from John Coker

(Above) Here's Knott's Berry Farm's prized No. 40 back when she still had her own small role in everyday Rocky Mountain railroading. As Rio Grande No. 340, she is seen with a short stock car train north of Ridgeway on the D&RGW during one of her final runs in the late summer of 1950. That's the majestic San Juan range in the background. This photographer didn't leave his name on the print, but he sure deserves credit for recording such a fine atmosphere. No. 340's last assignment was on the light Ouray branch, where she spent most of the time out of service as a standby for regular No. 318, thus this photo is all the more valuable. The Baldwin Consolidation went to work originally as D&RG No. 400 in May, 1881, just three months ahead of Knott's No. 41, which was built as D&RG No. 409. It is of great historical credit to Walter Knott that he had the foresight to save the pair of them together, along with some of their cars and other things. Who knows what further tales may yet be told of them.
Photo, John Coker Collection

N de M
In the Heart of Mexico City

There wasn't too much left of Mexico's once-vast network of three-foot gauge railroads by the mid-1960s, yet it was way more than could be seen by a couple of time and money-short young fellows intent on spending most of their meager energies on the narrow gauge further south in Guatemala. In the late 1800s, General William Palmer had in mind to provide narrow gauge service clear through from Denver, though he only managed to connect Mexico City with El Paso. At the end of WWII there were still some 1,100 miles of such trackage, but by the time of our visit in July 1964 that had shrunk to 324 miles, all of it on secondary routes running at a loss and due for abandonment. At least a week could have been used just to ride the remaining passenger and mixed trains; instead - and only by arranging our schedule carefully - we managed to spend most of one single day on this line.

The heart of Mexico's narrow gauge empire had always been in the capital city, so we went there to see what was left of it. Word was out that strangers were not welcome at the roundhouse and yard in San Lazaro, near downtown, but you could hang around the neighborhood and get shots of whatever trains came and went. We tried this in the early morning, but found that most of the steam activity took place behind a long, tall wooden fence. As young adventurers are wont to do, we wandered ever further within the confines of that fence, expecting to hear the word, "vamos" at any time, but finding ourselves mostly ignored.

(Left) The fence and a major highway are just off to the right. We have managed to reach a string of parked locomotives; I have climbed up into the cab of one, figuring to take a couple of quick overall shots before being seen and evicted. Out of despair I would have settled for this single picture, showing four live 2-8-0s, plus the one whose tender is in the foreground. No. 76 is the next one behind, while No. 256 is backing up on the adjacent track. That cloud of smoke from her stack came down as a fine sticky mist that noticeably aged a brand-new grey cowboy hat I'd bought at an open shop on the way here, a bit earlier. Some welcome!

(Opposite top) We soon learned that whatever policy there may have been, on this day no one cared if we walked around taking pictures. Maybe the hat was the right offering (the event had been duly noticed and was gleefully passed around). At any rate, here's 2-8-0 No. 255 backing away from the 10-stall roundhouse. N de M (National de Mexico) had about 40 locomotives left on its narrow gauge roster at this time, mostly built by Baldwin. This engine dates from 1899.

(Opposite, lower left) Shopwork was decidedly primitive, yet this old 2-8-0 is getting a major overhaul in one of the roundhouse stalls.

(Lower right) Here's No. 256 again - also an 1899 veteran - taking water while facing the turntable and roundhouse.

Both pages, AHW photos

(Below) Pemex tank car No. 1561 spent many years in the Colorado Rockies before its sale to Mexico in the 1940s. Airplane fans may want to get magnifying glasses to study the prop and early jet fighters parked over the fence and across the highway.

(Above) As a diesel fireman on leave of absence from work, I couldn't resist this view of steam taken from the fireman's seat showing N de M narrow gauge yard switcher No. 145 clanking past with a lot of huffing and hissing.

(Above right) Here's No. 145 again, handling standard gauge cars on dual gauge trackage. Built in 1904, this was one of the lightest engines left in service. Ironically, Mexico's heavier narrow gauge power was often scrapped first because it worked the busiest routes, which were converted to standard gauge. The remaining lines at the end had mostly 40 pound rail, thus a lot of the elderly, light engines were still on hand at the time of our visit. The OM on No. 145's tender is not meant as a mantra, but represents the engine's original home on the Mexican Eastern RR.

(Right) Four narrow gauge engines doze at San Lazaro shops while a fifth, No. 256, rumbles past with a string of standard gauge boxcars. The train is running over the dual gauge mainline to an industrial area further out of town. Among engines in the scene are Nos. 284, 255 and 76.

(Below left) The effects of earthquakes and old age were obvious at San Lazaro, with the brick, three-track shop building in back missing the centre part of its roof, though cars and engines were still being repaired inside. Shop crane in the foreground was made by Appleby Bros. of London. To the right sits the oil bunker from a tender.

(Below right) The visiting photographer gets more brave as the day goes by, here standing atop a standard gauge boxcar to catch this overall view of the San Lazaro dual gauge yard, with part of downtown Mexico City in the background. Yard fence and highway are at the right; two narrow gauge steamers are seen at work doing yard switching.
Both pages, AHW photos

(Opposite) Towards downtown from the roundhouse and shops was N de M's San Lazaro station, the big, red, brick, two-storey building seen in the background, said to have served some years ago as a leper hospital. No. 145 has just coupled up to heavier No. 270 in order to give the fairly long Puebla-bound passenger train some help getting out of town.

(Above) Typical of N de M's narrow gauge passenger car fleet was second class coach No. 984, seen here at San Lazaro after arriving with a mixed train. Clerestory-roofed cars were mostly first class coaches. Few of these have been saved, but some 20 of the engines were preserved, mainly because they were easy for N de M to transport to various Mexican parks and other display places.

(Right) Departure of the mixed train for Chipiltepec is seen from the balcony of a nearby old building. We were brought here by a young Mexican fellow who spoke little English but appeared to be a railfan. He sure gave us a ringside seat to narrow gauge railroading in downtown Mexico City. Rafael Blanco says this yard and station were demolished by mid-1970s, after narrow gauge operations ceased. On this site was built Mexico's new Parliament Building, which was then severely damaged by a 1989 fire. This was one of our final pictures here; I was so busy trying to compose a decent shot, with all the distractions, that I never checked the engine number until we got home and the film was developed. Looking in an N de M roster, I learned that here was the day's only non 2-8-0 engine, Ten-wheeler No. 185, built by Baldwin in 1924.

Both pages, AHW photos

(Opposite above) Southbound Train #110 (Mexico City to Cuautla) is seen at noon on July 4, 1962 north of Cuautla, Pueblo, Mexico.
(Opposite below) At Cuautla on the same day, we see FCI 2-8-0 No. 76 switching freight to go with the passenger cars in the background. The engine is lettered for N de M's Interocianico Division; it was built by Baldwin in 1900.

(Above) A week after the opposite scenes, the photographer has caught a narrow gauge freight train on the FCE arriving at Oriental, Puebla from Teziutlan.
(Right) Eastbound FCI Mixed train #254, operating between Puente de Ixtla and Cuautla, is seen leaving Cassasana on January 17, 1965.
Both pages, Elmer Treloar photos

A Guatemala Visit in 1964

An illustrated story in the April 1964 issue of **Trains** Magazine ("Narrow gauge, si! Steam locomotives, si, si!" by Frank Barry) made me realize that down in Guatemala there was one last chance to see American style narrow gauge steam railroading of the kind that fellows my age had missed out on by one or two generations. That is, Baldwin engines and wooden cars on mixed trains and mainline doubleheaders, roundhouses filled with active steam, branchlines, even connecting railroads with their own power. But time was a problem; between a full schedule of college courses plus employment as locomotive fireman on the Union Pacific RR, there was little chance for a" Central American holiday" (which happened to be the title of a little inspirational book by Gerald Best).

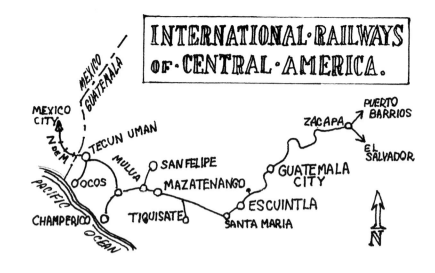

Nevertheless, by June 30 of that same year my friend Dave Riggle and I found ourselves in the Guatemalan border village of Tecun Uman, waiting to board an evening mixed train that would take us to Mazatenango on the first leg of a three day train trip to the country's capital. At school, it was summer vacation; also the U.P. superintendent gave me a week's leave of absence for "educational purposes," as he put it, being sympathetic to the real purpose of our trip.

On hindsight, perhaps we should have flown directly to Guatemala, instead of spending several of those precious days taking the slow and long route by train down from Mexico City, being distracted along the way by such things as NdeM steam (both standard and narrow gauge), antique steetcars in Veracruz, plus a pair of vacationing senoritas whose appeal was at least as strong as the trains to this pair of 20-year olds. A telegram sent from one of the railroad stations along the way advised the superintendent that I'd be a couple of days later than expected, but even that didn't give us time to catch more than a brief glimpse of an operation that was just then beginning to make its final steam showing.

(Below) It was raining at the border town of Tecun Uman when we entered Guatemala by walking across Rio Suchiate from Mexico over a long railroad and pedestrian bridge that brought us to a land of narrow gauge, narrow dirt roads and many burro trails. We bought tickets at the station window for Mazatenango, nearest place with a proper hotel, then sat under some trees nearby to enjoy fresh coconuts with others, bought from a trackside vendor. Near departure time we tackled the rain for a quick inspection of our train - a mixed with two tanks, four wooden boxcars, a baggage-mail car and four rapidly-filling coaches. To our surprise, a breakdown in the usual mainline 2-8-2 motive power gave us instead this handsome Baldwin 2-8-0, the 1910-built No. 71, which worked the two-hour trip to Mazatenango, where a heavier engine was already being steamed up in the roundhouse to take over our train.

International Railways of Central America

Central America's largest and best-known railroad at the time of our 1964 visit was the U.S. owned, three-foot gauge International Railways of Central America (IRCA), most of whose varied and interesting American-style equipment was lettered for the Spanish version of the same name, FIdeCA. Some 500 miles of this company's 800 mile system was within Guatemala, running from the Mexican border and a couple of Pacific coast ports to the Atlantic coast at Puerto Barrios, via the capital Guatemala City.

Justo Rufino Barrios is credited with getting railroads started in Guatemala, being himself at the engine's throttle of the first train into the capital in 1884. Unfortunately, as president of the country and its leading General, he was killed the following year when invading El Salvador to force it to join his proposed Central American Republic. A bronze monument to his memory has long adorned the front of the railroad's station and headquarters in Guatemala City.

Originally, Guatemala had a number of small private railroads, such as the Guatemala Central R.R., the Occidental R.R. and the Ocos R.R., but in 1912 these were consolidated into the Guatemala Railway, later changed to the IRCA. By the early 1960s this company's roster included 84 steam locomotives, 13 diesels, 209 passenger cars, 2,081 freight cars and 457 cars for company service. The whole line was to have been dieselized in 1960 at a cost of $11 million, but the financing could not be found.

Although providing important services for local people along its lines, the IRCA's main purpose was to move bananas from vast plantation holdings of the United Fruit Company to ships at coastal ports. Due to financial and political problems, that company began to curtail its operations about the time we were there, leading to the IRCA's bankruptcy soon after. Other private owners then tried to run the line for profit but failed, so the government took over in 1970 and renamed it Ferrocarril de Guatemala (Railroad of Guatemala) or FEGUA. Most of the branch lines were shut down, as was the international connection with El Salvador. A fleet of diesels then replaced most steam.

Recently the remaining line was sold to private investors from the U.S. and Mexico for a reported $25 million, but its future does not look very promising since much of the country's traffic now moves by cars and trucks. About a dozen steam locomotives remain on hand, most inoperable but one or two used on occasional charter and special trips.

(Above) We arrived after dark at a hotel near trackside in Mazatenago, listening to our train whistle off and blast out of town in the continuing rain. A good sleep was interrupted early by the sounds of two or three engines moving around in the yard nearby. Down at the station I learned (through poor Spanish) that two freights had come and gone while I was getting dressed, though more trains were due in the next hours. A short walk to the roundhouse area brought me to three engines being serviced for branchline runs, including 1904 Baldwin-built 2-6-0 No. 80, whose sister 81 was pictured in the *Trains* article. When I showed this to the engineer (standing in the gangway), he called someone else to see; before long there was a small crowd, one of whom asked me to take *their* picture. While I focused the camera, a local newspaperboy stopped by, hoping to make a sale. Even a carman in the background stopped to get into the view. Note the roundhouse welder holding the magazine.
(Below) IRCA Nos. 79, 80 and 81 were a trio of little Baldwin 32-ton Moguls based at Mazatenango in 1964 specifically to work the light rails and bridges of the San Felipe branch.
Both pages, AHW photos

(Above) This photo (and the coloured one on the front cover, taken a few moments earlier) is my consolation prize for two grand missed opportunities. On planning this trip to Guatemala, I yearned to ride one of the branchline mixed trains, but time and logistics were against it. Schedules and reliable information for them were hard to get and faciltiies were said to be almost nonexistant at their destinations. I felt lucky to at least see some of the branchline engines being serviced, their assigned crews being obviously proud of them. This was especially true of 2-8-0 No. 108, which had recently arrived from the IRCA's El Salvador division after an overhaul in Guatemala City. Before long I found myself in her cab with the fireman, who took me for a distant brother when he learned that I had the same occupation back in the U.S. He stared long at pictures of the modern yellow diesels that I worked on, while steam pressure built up on his engine and the fire roared. Then he invited me to ride with him down the branch to Champerico, where they were headed. I hestitated with longing, so he sweetened the offer by suggesting the engineer might let me run the engine part of the way. It was a chance I had to pass and never got again, though I rode along for a few hundred feet when they went for their train - a boxcar, a baggage-mail car and a single coach - after which I said goodbye and walked down the track some ways to set up for pictures of their departure. Of the three cameras I had with me, I usually saved the best scenes for my larger format 2 1/4 x 3 1/4 Speed Graphic, planning on good sharp enlargements. In this case I wanted to pan the engine as it went by me, using slow speed so that the counter balances would be blurred going around. I shot a colour slide first - never thinking it would be a future book cover - then grabbed this shot with an old WW II Exakta, my backup 35 mm camera, before putting my main effort into the moving scene. Regrettably, there was a problem with the big camera's focal plane shutter, resulting in 124 blank sheets of film when I got home from the trip. I not only missed my branchline mixed train cab ride, but also the picture I most wanted. Instead, I have this one showing the engine with throttle wide open for the uphill charge out of town, her engineer busy with the sanders as the wheels start to slip, while down below his cab flames shoot from the firebox and up ahead black clouds of smoke belch into the overcast, rainy sky. My new friend, the fireman, waves me a first and last goodbye; I can only imagine what it might have been like to spend the day up there with him.
AHW photo.

San Felipe

(This page) "What might have been!" says the photographer on the back of his print. "This 3 foot gauge 2-6-0 was given to me for the Colorado Railroad Museum, but political turmoil at the time kept me from getting it out of the country. The Japanese were paying $30 a ton for scrap steel, so the military cut up everything it could, including all three of the Moguls at Mazatenango, after the government took over the railroad and abandoned the branch.

"Riding and exploring a branch line in Guatemala was complicated. For instance, this San Felipe train didn't make connection with either of the mainline trains, so you had to stay over at Mazatenango and then persuade a reluctant taxi driver to tackle the road to Mulua, where you could catch this train.

"The rear coach at the time we rode was exhibiting its age in strange ways. Standing on the back platform and glancing down the aisle past the jammed-in passengers and all their typical Guatemalan luggage of vegetables, children, chickens, etc., it was observed that as the front end entered a curve that portion of the car leaned with the curve while the rear portion might still be tilting in the opposite direction.

"Facilities at San Felipe were simple - a combined freight and passenger station, a small yard and a turntable. This was probably little changed since the line was opened in 1894 from the port of Champerico, 54 miles away. San Felipe was briefly the junction of two railroads, after German capital built a rugged 80 mile electric line from here to Quezaltenango, which was some 8,000 feet higher up. Slides and storms wiped this line out a mere two years later. A pair of now rare postal stamps were issued at the time to commemorate this 'Ferrocarril Los Altos'."

Both, Robert W. Richardson photos

(Left) One wouldn't mistake Mulua for a busy place even at train time, seen here at 9:18 a.m. on January 25, 1965, yet the place was an important junction on the Guatemala mainline. Mogul No. 79 has just taken water after arriving light from Mazatenango, about 10 miles away, and is now waiting for Train M204, the Champerico-Tiquisate mixed, which will arrive behind a 2-8-0 or 2-8-2. After some switching, No. 79 will head up a light-tracked branchline to San Felipe, trailing three or four of #204's cars uphill on grades to 3.4%.

(Far left) It's now three minutes past noon and No. 79 has already been to San Felipe with her three-car mixed train, known as M201. At Mulua the train will be wyed, so that the baggage car is up front again, then No. 79 will bring it to Mazatenago, where the road engine is waiting.

(Right) The train is again M204, heading away from Mulua down the mainline with two boxcars added to the consist, but still hauled by the little 2-6-0. The road engine has gone ahead to Mazatenago, where it is being serviced while waiting for its train.
All three, Elmer Treloar photos.

(Above) Wood burning Mogul No. 6 of the IRCA forerunner Ferrocarril Occidental de Guatemala, built by Baldwin the 1899, was named for the remoted junction she served - "Mulua."
AHW collection

Escuintla

We rode the night time mixed train from Mazatenango to Escuintla; three coaches, a baggage car, two tankers and a boxcar, led by Mikado No. 204. Arriving at the dimly lit Escuintla depot long after dark, we were greeted by a pleasant mother and daughter whom we'd never met before, but who led us from our train to their simple dwelling on the far side of town, where their small house had an addition in which they rented rooms. You can sit back at this point and imagine that you're reading a novel, but it's actually a true story of life on the narrow gauge as experienced by my friend and I. Let me assure you it was a memorable night, too! For a start, they made up our beds, then departed very quickly and let us fight it out with tough mattresses and bothersome little creatures of various sorts.

(Left) Here's Escuintla as seen by brakeman and conductor of the daily passenger train bound from the Mexican border to Guatemala City. The station is back on the right, nine-stall roundhouse just beyond the left brakeman's hat. It's only 47 miles from here to the capital, but there are steep grades and sharp curves along much of the route.

emala	Guatemala	1	21
mplona	Pamplona	2	22
Eureka	Eureka	3	23
Gordo	Cerro Gordo		
o Seco	Campo Seco	4	
Frutal	Frutal	5	25
ngenio	Ingenio	6	26
Morán	Morán		
Zapote	Zapote	7	27
Laguna	Laguna		
l Paso	Mal paso	8	28
treras	Contreras	9	29
atitlán	Amatitlán	10	30
npañía	Compañía		
Llano	Llano	11	31
Palin	Palin	12	32
rmela	Carmela	13	33
eralda	Esmeralda		
Monte	Medio Monte	14	34
ando	San Fernando		
nás	Santo Tomás	15	35
	Concepción	16	36
	Escuintla	17	37
	Mauricio		
os	Corritos	18	38
xtán	Mixtán	19	39
Maria	Santa Maria		
asagua	Masagua	20	40
áquina	Máquina		
lhauer	Keilhauer		
Cádiz	Cádiz		
duardo	San Eduardo		
aranjo	Naranjo		
Obero	Obero		
Luisa	Santa Luisa		
Linares	Linares		
Larga	Montaña Larga		
rizona	Arizona		
José	San José		

Nulo si el corte que lleva la proyección no corre paralelo a la línea que señala la flecha.

FERROCARRILES INTERNACIONALES DE CENTRO AMERICA (División Guatemala)

Válido por un pasaje sin escalas, de la estación y en la fecha estampadas al dorso, hasta la estación indicada en la proyección cortada. NULO si no tiene PROYECCION mostrando destino.

Form B-27

SERIE A   Nº 16286

"ENTERO PRIMERA CLASE"

Hogger of the Narrow Gauge Mallet

(Above) Wandering through the yard at Escuintla early the morning after our arrival, a plume of moving smoke on the other side of some boxcars caught my eye. The engine making it was so small and moved so lightly that there was barely any chuffing, just the occasional clanking of rods. When it got out into the open, the engineer saw me, camera in hand, so he suddenly yanked open the throttle, giving me this show of smoke and steam.

It was No. 65, the Escuintla yard goat, switching cars to make up the next train. A trim little Baldwin 2-8-0 built in 1909, the machine was a pleasure to behold, tall silver stack and smokebox front adding to the regal appearance of a shiny black boiler, cab and tender. When they stopped near me again, the engineer waved that I should come aboard, so I quickly climbed into the very crowded cab. The whole crew was aboard, ready for a short run up the line to a coffee warehouse. The invitation was to ride along, our schedule allowing me this time to say yes.

The hogger's name was Jesus (with the J pronounced like an h), a friendly fellow with clipped silver mustache and a gold tooth in front, plus an old hat contoured by much rain and steam. He spoke English fairly well and said he was the senior engineer in town. His wife was ailing, so he'd lately bid on this switching job, but before then his assigned engine was No. 250, one of the famous Uintah/Sumpter Valley 2-6-6-2 Mallets. The pair was right then sitting across the yard from us, one being repaired under an open air shed, the other supplying parts (its boiler supposedly home to a poor local fellow). I was excited by this information and asked him how he'd liked that engine. "Oh, she was the son of a whore," he said without emotion, "much harder to run than the others, more places to oil, easy to come off the tracks; things were always coming loose or breaking." He said the curves in their tracks were hard on a machine that long. "But she sure could pull!" he swore. "Once we had 60 cars with her; I think she would have taken more, but they would have torn apart. Then we had troubles with her on the last trip; they sent another engine out to bring us in. When I got to town, that's when I learned my wife was sick. Since then that big engine hasn't run either."

Finca Concepcion

(Above left) Coffee, sugar and bananas grow in abundance around Escuintla, with one nearby plantation rumored to have its own little steam powered railroad. When we asked engineer Jesus aboard No. 65, he said the place was called Finca Concepcion and that we could walk there from the warehouse that we were going to switch. A 15 minute path through the jungle brought us into a clearing with this little tank engine steaming off to one side, the line's No. 1, an 0-4-2. It didn't take long for our arrival and interest to become known, with employees and their families living right beside the train tracks which wound in and out among warehouses and processing buildings, then headed into the sugar plantation beyond. A few workers came out to greet us, but they said the day's work had already finished; the engine was shut down.

(Above) Parked a few yards behind the little steamer was another, this one No. 2 and under repair. Closer inspection revealed them both to have come from the German builder Orenstein & Koppel in the 1920s. One fellow was inside No. 2 slowly banging away at some of the tubes, while two others stood outside and kept him company, now and then handing in something. They said the headlight came from a standard gauge engine in Mexico. Note the short boiler tubes on the ground.

(Left) Finca Concepcion had the most lightweight railroad operation I've run into, as evidenced here by the "big hook." This little woodburning rig was parked near the engine track.

Wooding-Up

(Above) This was our lucky day! Someone in the crowd went off to get the engineer (the middle aged fellow nearest to the engine), who came back smiling and asked if we wanted to see her run. Guess he didn't want to disappoint visitors with cameras from so far away. Our enthusiastic response led to some quick orders, after which a crew of five fueled the little tanker up. As a student of old time railroading, this was a scene I've often imagined but got to experience just this once. Then the engineer called us up into the cab for a quick cruise around the mill grounds, plus a brief photo runby. That was fun, but nothing could top this timeless scene right here, which for me was worth the whole trip to Guatemala by itself. Incidentally, we later found out that few photographers ever reached Finca Concepcion; those who did usually found the bigger No. 2 steaming, not No. 1.

Both pages, AHW photos

(Above left) Among narrow gauge railroading's most famous locomotives were the IRCA's No. 250 and sister 251, seen here in 1964 shortly after they were taken out of service at Escuintla. Built by Baldwin in 1928 as 2-6-6-2T Nos. 50 and 51 for Colorado's Uintah Railway, they were the only three foot gauge Mallets to serve in the United States, spending several years on Oregon's Sumpter Valley line after the Uintah was closed down in 1938. Originally coal burning tank engines, they later used fuel oil and had tenders. Attempts to bring these engines back to further fame in the U.S. moved slower than the Guatemalan military's scrap drive, though at this writing the tenders still exist.

(Below left) Business car "Michitoya" brings up the rear end of today's northbound passenger train, stopped at Escuintla on its way to the Mexican border. Although the mainline still runs through here, the roundhouse, water tank and other structures were abandoned with the end of steam service in the early 1970s.

(Above) Due to an impending bout of "Montezuma's revenge," (picked up from an ice cream vendor a couple hours earlier) this was my last photo out on the IRCA's mainline. Business car "Michitoya" is at the head end of the daily passenger train running from Escuintla to Guatemala City. We are picking up speed to attack the steepest grade on the entire line, three miles of 3.7% going up Palin Hill, which required helpers out of Escuintla on most trains. After that we had four scenic miles along the shores of Lake Atitlan, followed by DeSola, which at 5,009 feet was the highest point on the system, a short three miles from Guatemala City's downtown station - and relief in a clean hotel room!

All three, AHW photos

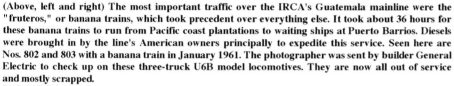

(Above, left and right) The most important traffic over the IRCA's Guatemala mainline were the "fruteros," or banana trains, which took precedent over everything else. It took about 36 hours for these banana trains to run from Pacific coast plantations to waiting ships at Puerto Barrios. Diesels were brought in by the line's American owners principally to expedite this service. Seen here are Nos. 802 and 803 with a banana train in January 1961. The photographer was sent by builder General Electric to check up on these three-truck U6B model locomotives. They are now all out of service and mostly scrapped.
Both, C.S. Rumsey photos

(Below left) Mikado meets Consolidation to create this mishap in Zacapa yard during 1949.
(Below right) Results of a worse derailment are seen somewhere out on the line back in 1950, when the lack of cranes and heavy machinery was made up for by manpower with block and tackle, both seen at the front of No. 195.
Both photos, AHW collection

In the Backshop

(Above left) Not many narrow gauge railroads anywhere in the world boasted more extensive shops than the IRCA at Guatemala City. A visit to the railroad's offices the morning after our arrival from Escuintla led to an invitation by Superintendent Thornton (from the U.S., like other officials back then) to join him for a tour of the shops. Beginning at the turntable near the mainline, we followed a track right through the 18 stall roundhouse into Backshop No. 1, seen here from the overhead crane, where four Mikados were receiving major overhauls. Three of these engines were Baldwins, while the third from front is a Krupp. Workmen were busy inside them, replacing tubes and firebricks, while others worked on running gear, cabs, piping and domes. Blacksmiths and machinists in Backshop No. 2 made most of the required parts right on the spot.
AHW photo

(Below left) Guatemala City shop crews were especially proud of the cosmetic overhaul they gave to the IRCA's oldest engine, 4-4-0 No. 84, seen here on the transfer table between Backshop No. 1 and 2. Last of its type on the railroad, this Eight-wheeler spent its final years on the Mexican border, often working the 40-pound rails of the Ocos branch, else as the Tecun Uman yard switcher. In a fresh coat of dark green paint, with grey smokebox and stack, plus red trim and gold lettering, its brass parts nicely polished, the engine was headed for park display in the railroad's corporate home of New York City just a few months before our 1964 visit. Sometime later, however, the 1876 Baldwin was discovered to be a true historical gem, having operated originally out of Santa Cruz, California. Thereupon she was moved to the Smithsonian Institution, given a complete rebuilding, then placed on an indoor pedestal for her final rest.
AHW collection

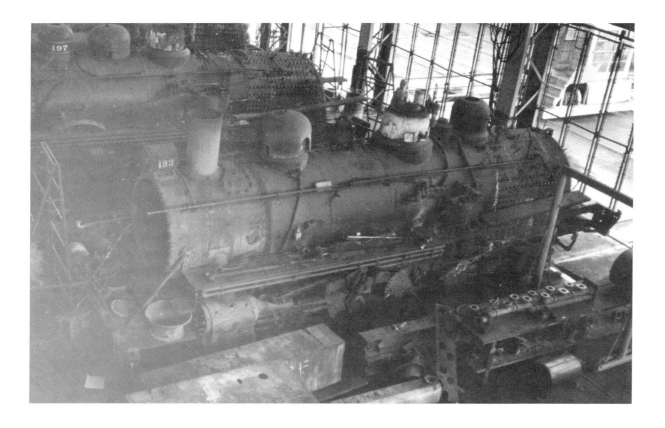

(Above left) Looking down at Baldwin 2-8-2 No. 193 from Backshop No. 1's overhead crane, which the operator delighted in showing off with the boss' permission. A pair of 2-8-0s sat outside the shop waiting to go in next for major repairs. As long as the IRCA depended on steam, the two locomotive backshops were kept very busy. An electric winch and cable regularly moved engines between these two on the the transfer table seen in the background. Shop No. 3 employed many carpenters to keep the wooden car fleet in good repair, while Shop No. 4 was for the construction of new rolling stock, mainly steel framed banana cars, with iron sides and roofs. Fittings for these were shipped down from the U.S. Incidentally, a steady sideline for the carpenters was the building of wooden cowcatchers for most of the engines. We even found carpenters rebuilding two wooden boxcars in the open air outside the shops, so busy was this whole place in 1964.
AHW photo

(Below left) Ten-wheelers were still common power, especially on mixed trains, when this photo was taken outside the Guatemala City shops in May 1952. No. 98 was built by Baldwin in 1901, one of Ten 4-6-0s then on the roster. During our trip we saw three of them, one each as standby power in the roundhouses at Mazatenango and Escuintla, with the third one missing parts and headed for scrap. None of these engines survived.
Railway Negtaive Exchange/AHW collection

(Right) One of the first cars to receive the new two-tone green paint scheme of the mid-1960s was the steel bodied "Michitoya" seen here at Escuintla, heading north on an inspection trip in 1964. Note the brass railing and canvas awning on the back platform.
AHW photo

(Lower right) New coach G106 features steel construction, but with such vintage details as truss rods and open end, as seen outside the Guatemala City shops on December 24, 1959. The photographer says, "It was proposed to build some for the D&RGW's 'Silverton,' which would have brought an interesting international flavour to the Rockies. The Rio Grande ended up building a new set of cars in its own Denver shops, soon after this."
R.W. Richardson photo

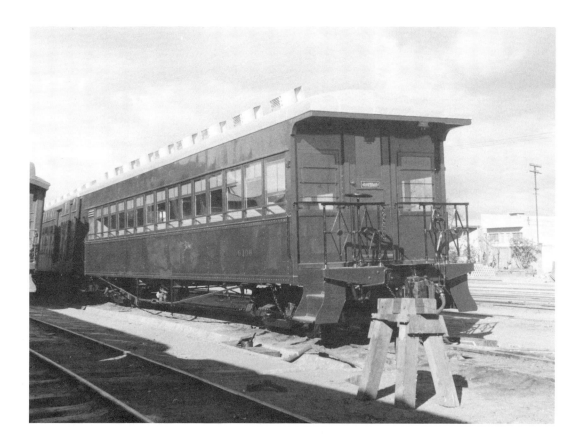

	Mazatenango	1	21
on	Chitalón	2	22
Rosal	Rosal	3	23
aguilar	Aguilar	4	24
enango	Cuyotenango	5	25
iguansis	Siguansis	6	26
Maricón	Maricón	7	27
ebastián	San Sebastián	8	28
alhuleu	Retalhuleu	9	29
Cuchilla	La Cuchilla	10	30
ndelaria	Candelaria	11	31
s Cruces	Las Cruces	12	32
oronado	Coronado	13	33
Reposito	Reposito	14	34
Animas	Las Animas	15	)
Miguelito	San Miguelito	16	36
Alianza	Alianza	17	37
Génova	Génova	18	38
Auyón	Auyón	19	39
lortensia	Hortensia	20	40
speranza	Esperanza		
atepeque	Coatepeque		
Dalmacia	Dalmacia		
e Grande	Monte Grande		
Pilar	Pilar		
s Palmas	Las Palmas		
Triunfo	Triunfo		
lo Ancho	Vado Ancho		
Pajapita	Pajapita		
leléndrez	Meléndrez		
El Prado	El Prado		
n Umán	C. Tecún Umán		

Nulo si el corte que lleva la proyección no corre paralelo a la línea que señala la flecha.

SERIE A   Nº 50473

FERROCARRILES INTERNACIONALES DE CENTRO AMERICA
(División Guatemala)

Válido por un pasaje sin escalas, de la estación y en la fecha estampadas al dorso, hasta la estación indicada en la proyección cortada. NULO si no tiene PROYECCION mostrando destino.

ENTERO
PRIMERA CLASE

Agente de Fletes y Pasajes

Nulo si el corte que lleva la proyección no corre paralelo a la línea que señala la flecha.

IRCA
Passenger Cars

(Right) One of the IRCA's finest pieces of rolling stock is the 30 foot wooden business car "Motagua" seen here out of service at Guatemala City in 1964. Inside, it had a galley, icebox, shower and berths for four, plus the rear observation area. Painted dark green, it was said to have a turn-of-the-century American background. I would have preferred this portrait without the political graffiti; better yet, with the car hooked behind one of the smaller engines.

(Centre) IRCA 141 was serving as a trackside medical dispensary at the time of this 1964 photo, though in its earlier years it was said to have been a coach on North Carolina's Tweetsie R.R.

(Below) Typical of the older style wooden passenger cars on the IRCA - built to American narrow gauge plans into the 1940s - was second class coach No. G170. Most wooden cars were scrapped after IRCA's government takeover and branchline abandonments. Of special note is the survival of one wooden coach, rebuilt and now serving as private quarters for crane operators, carrying the Spanish name for "Skinny Cat."

All three, AHW photos

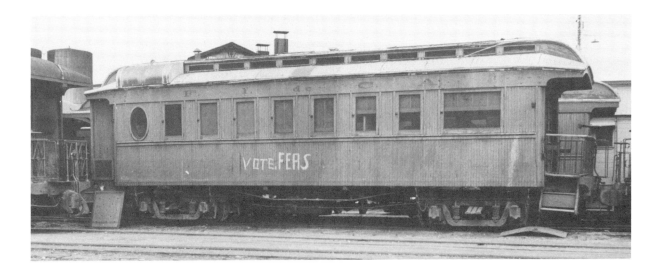

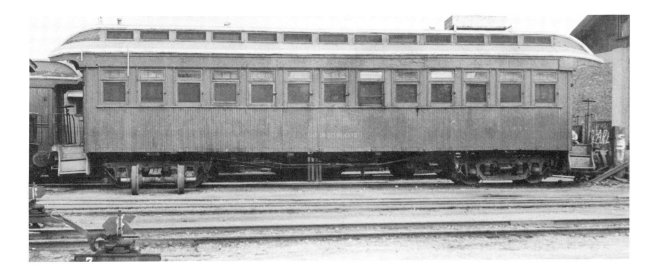

Guatemalan Cabooses

(Above and above left) Side-door cabooses were pretty rare on any railroad by 1964; this is the only one we saw in Guatemala. It was yellow with green trim and may have been rebuilt from a standard boxcar. There's a date of 11-58 on the lower right hand side, though this could refer to a rebuilding rather than when it was new. The Escuintla yard switcher had just hooked it to the rear of a northbound freight. Note that there are no end platforms.

(Left) This is the standard 3-window caboose used on most IRCA freights, even to this day. The G in front of its number shows its assignment within Guatemala.

AHW photos

(Left) Carpenters in Guatemala City's car shops were kept busy repairing the large wooden fleet that served in moist, tropical climates. In this case, one of the standard cabooses is getting a major rebuild.

(Lower left) One of the more unique pieces of equipment on the IRCA was Cummins diesel powered No. 515, said to have been built as a paymaster's car, but also serving officials for occasional inspection trips. It was painted dark green with a silver roof, like the passenger equipment.

(Below) Speeder No. 538 served as an ambulance, mainly to bring medical help from Guatemala City to outlying locations.

All three AHW photos

(Above) IRCA No. 298 was the smallest unit on the railroad's roster, built by Whitcomb for industrial service, seen here ready to depart Guatemala City with a weed-spraying train. The two men riding upstairs at the back must have gotten their fill of chemical fumes.

AHW collection

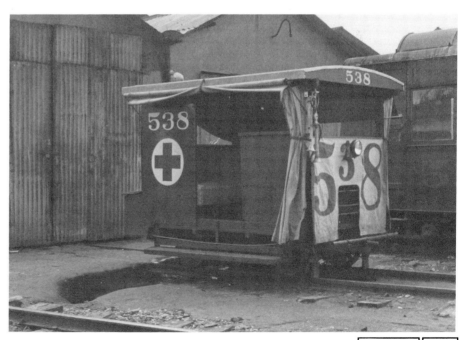

(Above) "Ten of a Kind" or, the "House of Mikes." Ten 2-8-2 narrow gauge engines wait for the call to duty in downtown Guatemala City, at the IRCA's 18-stall roundhouse. It was our last day before flying home and we saw so much steam operation that it was impossible to keep up with it all. In addition, time, film, and money had practically run out for us. It was one of those experiences that on hindsight could have benefitted from a great deal more time and energy - not to mention modern lenses and good fast film, plus a tripod for some night scenes. One of the hostlers is seen dressed in white, grooming up because he's going over to meet the passenger train and bring its engine to the roundhouse. This was a friendly place, where railroad photographers were welcome.

(Below) The roundhouse was busy that August day in 1964. This was the third engine within minutes to ride the turntable. Another of them is seen at the left, backing to the standpipe for water, before heading out of town as helper on an eastbound freight. The train's lead engine already went out a while ago and No. 188 will be the second helper. It is the first-three engine train we've encountered on our trip, but right here in the curving yard we won't really be able to see it. The ideal would have been to rent a taxi for a couple of dollars and ride to the edge of the city for shots of the train crossing that immense trestle seen on other pages. But time was too short for that - the train was not due to leave for an hour yet and by then we were on our way to the airport. Due to the convoluted politics of Guatemala over the years, various names and markings have adorned the equipment. In this case, Baldwin-built 2-8-2 No. 188 carries the name CIA AGRICOLA on its tender, which means it ran originally on the United Fruit Company's railroads, which were starting to decline. However, engines and cars were regularly shifted around between the railroad and the banana company, since both operated from the same U.S. background and control.

(Top right) Other than a pair of heavy yellow road units coming into Guatemala City's yard with a freight, this was the only diesel action we saw on our trip! General Electric No. 701 was yellow and black, standing out among the dark green passenger cars and mostly-red freight. Ironically, within 24 hours I would find myself back at work on a unit of vaguely similar style and colours, in the heart of another big city, much further north, on a much bigger gauge.

When I talked to one of the firemen about this, we compared wages. For a basic day on a yard engine I was given 100 miles, or $21 in pay. This fellow usually worked much less miles on the light narrow gauge trains but at much longer hours, for which he received two queztals, which bought about the same as two dollars back home. It was then that the name and theme of "Banana republic" became clear to me for the first time in my life. Foreign interests controlled both the railroad and the main business for it, bananas, plus the purse and powers of the country.

(Right) This was my farewell shot in Guatemala, clean Baldwin-built 2-8-2 No. 204 being brought to the roundhouse after arriving at the capital city with the passenger train from the Mexican border. Boy, that's a fine looking machine, the-third last steam engine built for the IRCA, new in 1948 only 16 years earlier. What's more, this engine survives and is used on occasional charter trains. It is said to be the most original of the line's dozen surviving steamers.

Both pages, AHW photos

Elmer Treloar
Visits Guatemala

Among the few dozen seriously dedicated photographers to document the final era of North American steam railroading was Elmer Treloar, whose well composed scenes were regularly published in RAILROAD Magazine during the 1950s and 60s (along with occasionally-ascerbic letters about railroads and railfans who had rubbed him wrong). He made several trips to Guatemala, usually braving the rough, unmarked roads in rented cars to capture scenes not available to those like my friend and I who rode the trains.

(Left) One of Guatemala's most spectacular railroading sights continues to be Puente de las Vacas bridge, on the northern edge of Guatemala City, a silver painted spiderweb-looking affair that carries trains some 262 feet above the jungle floor. In steam days most trains had two or three engines, spaced some distance apart, sometimes even four. An adventurous photographer could wait in the downtown freight yard until the train was about ready to start, then rush out to the front of the depot for a taxi that would bring him fairly close to a viewing site like this one. A northbound freight has just left the city behind Krupp-built 2-8-2 No. 167 on September 30, 1967.

(Opposite) Approaching the city with a southbound train from Puerto Barrios, this freight has a Mike on the point and another cut in a few cars back. Look carefully for the white shirt of a "suicide jockey," one of the brakemen practicing the common Guatemalan custom of sitting on the upright brakewheel of a boxcar roof not far behind the engine. Considering that derailments were fairly common, these fellows were either brave or foolhardy. The date is October 2, 1967.

Both, Elmer Treloar photos

(Above) There's lots of steep railroading on the narrow gauge through Guatemala, such as the grade coming down to this bridge which the photographer reached by driving 27 kilometers north from the capital on Highway 9. He says Baldwin No. 203 is running northbound with Train #2, which is the daily passenger. Although this train usually ran as a mixed, on this day all we see are boxcars. If it does have coaches as well, they're sure out of sight.

(Right) The IRCA's more mountainous Atlantic division saw most freight trains running with helpers back in steam days, as seen here near the village of Chile, with two Mikados spaced out among the wooden boxcars on their way to Guatemala City in 1965. Another daring brakeman is enjoying his rooftop ride from a brakewheel seat near the second helper.

Zacapa to El Salvador

(Right) Zacapa was a dramatic place in steam days because the large, two story Hotel Ferrocarril was right at trackside near the big open-air engine shed, part of which is seen here with No. 183 inside. All rooms at the hotel came with live train sounds and window rattling, as the tracks were just outside. Mikado No.200 was among the last batch of steam engines built by Baldwin for the railroad in 1948. By the time of this December 1977 photo, the line had been renamed from IRCA to FEGUA (Ferrocarril Guatemala) and was generally dieselized, but some steam was kept on hand for charter train business. At this writing No. 200 is among a dozen steam engines still available, including three of the 2-8-0s.
Jim Dunlop photo

(Below) In the 1920s a noteworthy branchline was built south from the IRCA mainline at Zacapa to the border of El Salvador, going through a spectacular series of loops and 11 tunnels that brought trains way up steep mountainsides, at one point allowing passengers to look back down on six levels of tracks. Here's Mixed Train #21 at its southern destination, crossing from Guatemala into El Salvador shortly before noon on October 5, 1967. We are at the lonely frontier town of Angiatu, where soldiers and customs men with guns and suspicious glances are in complete charge, checking everything on the train. It was the same when crossing between Guatemala and Mexico; they were not good places in which to linger, especially with cameras, thus there are few photos of border train activity. Although the tracks are still in place, political convolutions mentioned elsewhere, along with a big decline in traffic, brought an end to train service on this branch around 1980. Since then, in a "back to the land" kind of spirit, some local services have been provided privately by various homemade speeders.
Both pages, Elmer Treloar photos

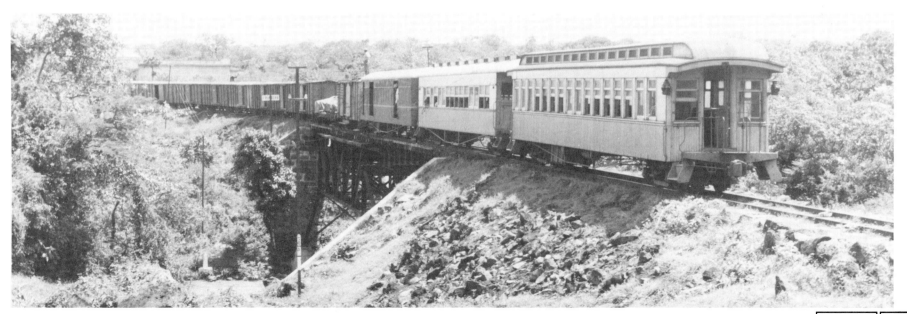

Through Guatemala in 1915

Here are some scenes from an anonymous fellow who travelled through Guatemala in 1915 by train and took a few Kodak snapshots along the way. He didn't leave his name, nor much information, just a little set of prints in a yellowed envelope, with the name of the country and a few locations written here and there. We could wish he had kept a diary, yet we're lucky to have any record from that era at all. Keep in mind, this is the next country south of Mexico, with a narrow gauge line following American prototype. Sort of a banana-hauling D&RGW, with beautiful Moguls, Consolidations and Mikados from Baldwin.

(Left) The photographer's train has arrived at Zacapa, an important terminal on the mainline route between Guatemala City and Puerto Barrios on the Atlantic coast. Zacapa is well known for its Hotel Ferrocarril, with rooms overlooking the tracks. Zacapa's station is of an interesting design used at several locations, the glassed observation tower being a unique feature.

(Below) The arid country around Zacapa is in stark contrast to dense jungle foliage along the railroad's Pacific portions. There is a windmill in the background for water, perhaps to serve the roundhouse at the right. The silver painted faces of at least three engines can be seen. The nearest wooden boxcar is lettered "Guatemala N. 1152," while the third one says "F.C.I.deC.A." This was before the country's network of narrow gauge lines was consolidated into the single I.R.C.A., the International Railways of Central America, also called F.I.deC.A. or Ferrocarriles Internationales de Centro America.

(Above left) The Hotel Ferrocarril in Zacapa was quite new at the time of this picture, though the station's warehouse at the right looks well used already. Boxcars and the nose of an engine are barely visible in between.

(Below left) Canyon bridge over Puente Fiscal was recorded from a speeding passenger train's back platform. Note the small white station at the other side.

(Above) The next station east of Zacapa was here in Gualan, where native crowds greet the arrival of a mixed train. In the days before steel tanks, a sizeable wooden water tower stands further down the line.

All photos, collection of John Poulsen

(Opposite, upper left) Narrow gauge street running in the heart of Guatemala City, with two much more primitive forms of transportion travelling on the big cobblestones.

(Upper right) Street running of a different sort is seen at this small village, where some substantial structures line the tracks.

(Left) Station stop of a Guatemalan mixed train trailing beautiful open-end chair car No. 18, which is simply lettered "Northern." The engine is probably a 2-8-0, heaviest power on the line at that time.

(Above) Light coloured clothing is certainly the style in this warm country, as Guatemalan 4-4-0 No. 4 pauses with her train at some unrecorded station whose three tracks are well on their way to becoming a part of the land. The car of logs next to the engine has link and pin couplers.

(Right) Here's No. 4 highballing across a trestle out of town, hauling an aging trio of baggage car andcoaches. This is thought to be the 1876 Baldwin 4-4-0 that originally worked on the California coast near Santa Cruz, then later became IRCA No. 84, and is now a thoroughly restored prize exhibit at the Smithsonian Institute in Washington, D.C.
All photos, collection of John Poulsen

(Above) Looks like a fresh-cut load of lumber going from the sawmill to a nearby standard gauge connection, with the whole family out for a trestle portrait - old folks, parents and a couple of kids, one of whom isn't even wearing shoes. That was often the intimate nature of narrow gauge railroading, built to serve local interests and operated with minimal pretensions. A note on the back of this old print says it might have been taken on the Michigan-California Lumber line near Pino Grande, although several other logging outfits in that part of the country used similar tankers to this Porter-built No. 1.
AHW collection

(Opposite) Ward Kimball gives a shot of oil to his own little Tanker, the 1883 Baldwin-built "Chloe," stopped in front of the Grizzly Flats station in San Gabriel, California about 1960. This scene shows the results of one man's determination to save examples of vintage narrow gauge railroading. Starting in 1937 with the purchase of a Carson & Colorado coach, Kimball spent the next 50 years assembling this narrow gauge museum in his own backyard. The engine came from a Hawaiian plantation, the 1875 switch stand from the DSP&P in Colorado, while the side-door caboose by the enginehouse was once owned by California's Pacific Coast Railway. Inside sat the prize of the collection, an 1881 Baldwin Mogul from the Nevada Central RR. Ward recently gave his Grizzly Flats Railroad to the nearby Orange Empire Railway Museum.
Photo from Ward Kimball